[JODY]

by JERRY HULSE

W. H. ALLEN · LONDON
N1   A Howard & Wyndham Company
1977

Printed and bound in Great Britain by
Butler & Tanner Ltd, Frome and London,
for the Publishers, W. H. Allen & Co. Ltd,
44 Hill Street, London W1X 8LB

ISBN 0 491 01988 2

Book design by Ingrid Beckman

For Jody and my mother

PREFACE

THIS IS A STORY about my wife, Jody, a true story. It is also the story of literally millions of un-named people whose identity is imprisoned by the label *adoptee*. The records of their parentage remain locked away in courthouses across the nation. Rarely are they ever revealed. When adoptees attempt to learn their origins, they are told the file has been sealed for the protection of all concerned. And so it goes: adoptee, adoptive parents, natural parents enshrouded in a cloak of secrecy. The past is erased, almost as if the birth had never occurred. But now others, like Jody, are demanding that they be told the truth, that the answer at last be given to the question: *Who am I?* Thousands have stepped forward to voice their protest, like one adoptee who wrote recently: "I am buried alive without rights. I'm entombed in a courthouse. I am sealed up just as if my true self had died at birth.

The judge is playing God. I have asked him to give me life, but he refuses. All I wish to know is . . . who am I? My life is a continuing mystery—there is a mountain of resentment building inside me. I am determined to know who I am. I would rather know the truth . . . no matter what it might be . . . than to be haunted by not knowing. But I won't give up. Some day I will learn the secret."

Perhaps the truth could be painful. Yet virtually all adoptees are willing to take that risk. The adopted brother of an acquaintance of mine spent ten years searching for his natural mother. When he found her, he discovered she was a drunk and a prostitute. Still adoptees insist the truth is less painful than the mystery. Whichever is the case, one fact stands clear: they want to know.

Just over a year ago I began a search for my wife's natural mother. It began with a medical emergency, and it took me thousands of miles before it ended in a small town in the Midwest. This is the story of a handful of people and what happened to them. It is also, I see now, the story of hundreds of thousands of Americans still seeking their own true names, each a nomad searching for the place in blood and in spirit from which he or she came. If you are adopted this may be your story, as in a sense it is also the story of every human being who has ever wondered about the heart's journey home.

JERRY HULSE
Los Angeles

1

TRAFFIC WAS FLOWING SMOOTHLY as the yellow Mustang swung onto the Hollywood Freeway. Glancing into the rearview mirror, Jody maneuvered the car cautiously into the second lane. Behind her a motorist slowed while she picked up speed, accelerating until the speedometer needle swept across the dial to 50. Relaxed, Jody leaned over to switch on the radio. As she touched the knob, her ears suddenly began ringing—she felt strangely light-headed, sick to her stomach. Her fingers went numb and she knew she was going to faint. Instinctively, she pulled her foot from the gas pedal, then reached down and snapped on the air conditioner. But not even the wash of cool air could stop her slow descent into a darkening world. Ahead, cars began disappearing in a crazy blur of color.

She felt the steering wheel spin in her hands. Cars

behind her skidded, their tires screeching as the yellow Mustang zigzagged from lane to lane, Jody slumped over in the seat now, utterly unconscious. Driverless, the car slammed into the divider. A bumper guard broke loose and the car careened wildly back across the highway, spun around, nearly overturned, struck the divider a second time, and then slid to a stop, blocking the third and fourth lanes.

It wasn't until a policeman opened the door and raised her head that Jody regained consciousness.

"Are you hurt?" he asked.

"No—no, I don't think so."

"Sure?"

"Yes . . . I think I'm sure."

He looked at her curiously. "What happened, lady?"

"I don't know. . . . I really don't know."

While traffic crawled by, a wrecker hooked onto the Mustang and towed it away. Jody rode home in a police car.

Two days later it happened again. I looked up from the newspaper and saw Jody staggering around the living room like a drunk.

I grabbed her. "Jody, what is it?"

"Nothing . . . I don't know . . . nothing, really."

"What do you mean, nothing? The way you were stumbling? Are you okay?"

"I just felt dizzy for a moment, that's all."

She reassured me she was all right. But the next day I heard her moaning in the back yard. She was watering the lawn and her legs had buckled; she'd fallen, striking her head on a sprinkler. Blood was running from the cut, and she'd injured her ankle.

"I'm afraid it's broken," she sobbed.

Our neighbor Katy Hoyt helped me carry Jody into the house, and I explained to Katy what had been going on.

"This is insane," Katy said. "Jody should see a doctor. It's madness, going on this way."

We helped Jody to the car, and I drove her to the emergency hospital. The doctor who X-rayed her ankle said that it was sprained, not broken.

"How did it happen?" he asked.

Jody told him about the dizziness. "It's strange . . . it came over me so suddenly. . . ."

He took her blood pressure. "How long have you been having these dizzy spells?" he asked.

"Several weeks," she admitted.

As he bandaged her ankle he urged Jody to get a complete physical examination. But Jody insisted it wasn't necessary.

"It's nothing," she argued, "just something to do with these headaches I'm having."

I protested. "Jody, please—"

But she shook her head. "I don't want to discuss it," she said.

And then Jody began to lose control of her left hand. She was constantly breaking dishes, dropping things. She couldn't understand why. She'd be dizzy in the morning, and still be dizzy at night.

She was visiting a friend shortly after her ankle healed and the room suddenly grew hazy.

"Mabel, I can't see your face . . . something is happening to my eyes . . . your face . . . it's disappearing!"

Slowly Mabel's face took shape again, the objects in the room sliding back into focus. Jody sat there trembling, frightened, terribly frightened. Was she losing her sight? Or her mind?

Later that day Jody visited an ophthalmologist, Dr. Edwin Wright. She told him how the dizziness was occurring with greater frequency, that she suffered blackouts, blurred vision. She described the accident on the freeway, and as she spoke the doctor placed a stethoscope to her neck. Afterwards he explained that there was a murmur in one of her arteries. It indicated a blockage, an obstruction that was interfering with the flow of blood.

The doctor spoke candidly. "Mrs. Hulse, you must see a vascular surgeon immediately. You are gravely ill."

Dr. Wright warned that unless Jody sought prompt medical treatment she would soon die of a stroke or become a hopeless cripple.

On the drive home I tried to comfort her. "We'll get help," I said. "We'll find a surgeon. . . ."

She began sobbing. "I'm so frightened."

I fought off a sudden impulse to turn the car around and drive to the nearest hospital, to insist that Jody be admitted on the spot. I squeezed her hand tightly. "I love you," I said.

She smiled weakly. "I love you, too."

At home I telephoned our internist, Dr. Webster Marxer. When I explained the gravity of Jody's illness he told me he would see her first thing the following day.

Jody was so dizzy the next morning I had to help her dress.

She tried to joke. "You'd better get a new model— the tread on me is wearing out, I guess."

I took her in my arms. "I'd get a million dollars on the trade-in."

We arrived at the medical building at eight-thirty. As Jody stepped into the elevator, her knees buckled and she slumped against the door. I reached for her and she fainted in my arms. I carried her into the doctor's office.

"Mrs. Hulse fainted," I shouted to the nurse. "Where's Dr. Marxer?" She ran to get the doctor while I made Jody comfortable on the waiting-room couch.

"Everything seems so blurred," Jody said weakly when she came to.

The examination was thorough. Dr. Marxer took her blood pressure and pulse, checked her eyes, her re- flexes, her respiration. Had she been feverish lately? "No." Was there any numbness of the hands? "Yes." Double vision? "Yes." Slurring of speech? "Yes."

He placed a stethoscope to her neck and listened.

At last he said, "Jody, the other doctor was right— there is an obstruction in one of the arteries. What this means is that your brain is not getting enough blood. You're going to have to be hospitalized . . . there is no other choice."

Jody's terror was immediate. "Dr. Marxer, I want to go home."

"Jody . . . I'm sorry."

He called to his receptionist, "Jackie, phone St. John's and request an emergency admission."

During the next five days Jody underwent a series of tests at the hospital. A neurologist placed coins in her hands.

"Close your eyes."

She could feel with the right hand but was unable to tell if she still held coins in her left hand.

The feeling in her left hand was gone.

A full battery of checks and probes followed: ultrasound studies, an arteriogram, an aortogram, and a renal arteriogram. Blood tests were made and she was given an electroencephalogram to determine whether there had been brain damage. None as yet. Finally Dr. Marxer read us the report. Jody was suffering from fibro-muscular hyperplasia of the internal carotid arteries. The carotid arteries carry blood from the heart to the brain, he explained. Any obstruction in the carotid arteries could bring instant death or a crippling stroke at any time. In Jody's case there was a blockage near the base of the brain. Only surgery could save her life.

And a full medical history would be necessary.

It was now that the question of heredity was mentioned. Had either of Jody's parents suffered a stroke? Were they still living? If not, at what age did they die? What about diabetes?

Jody stared at Dr. Marxer with a stunned expression. "I don't know. . . . I have no idea who I am," she said.

"I don't understand," Dr. Marxer said.

"I'm adopted," Jody said. "I don't know who my real parents are." Then, closing her eyes, she said, "Please, I don't want the operation."

Dr. Marxer took Jody's hand in his.

"I'm frightened," Jody said.

"I know," Dr. Marxer said.

"I'm very frightened," Jody said.

"Of course . . ." Dr. Marxer said, still holding her hand, "but you want to live."

The surgery would be performed a week from Friday, in nine days.

Outside in the hall I spoke with Dr. Marxer. "Is there an alternative?"

He shook his head. "No. None."

"How long will she live if she doesn't go through with this?"

"Six months. A year. A year at the most."

"Only a year?"

"Only a year. I'm sorry, Jerry." He stared at me. "Do you suppose you could find her family?"

Find Jody's family? Was it possible? Had I even found Jody? Always there had been a part of her I could never reach, a part of her she could not give, perhaps because she didn't have it to give . . . a woman without an identity.

"It's that important—finding her family?" I asked.

He nodded. "It's essential," he said. "Essential because we have no idea what we are working with. From a genetic standpoint, we're in the dark."

"And if I can find them . . . ?"

"First, I would like to learn if her parents are subject to blood vessel disease. It's particularly important to know if this is an inherited disease and, if so, whether in Jody's family's case it progresses slowly or rapidly."

Dr. Marxer looked at me evenly.

"It would be enormously helpful to Jody's morale if you could find her family. It could be a big boost." He paused. "She must fight hard to live. We're going in at the base of the skull. It's a delicate operation . . . she's a gravely ill woman. Jerry, let's do all we can to give her the will to pull through."

I left the hospital alone. A heavy fog had rolled in from the ocean, obscuring buildings and cars. I watched Jody's window for a long time, and then I saw the light go out. As a newspaper reporter, I'd worked on hundreds of stories, but this was going to be the one that counted.

2

THE NEXT MORNING I REACHED automatically for the clock. Six thirty. Time suddenly had become precious. Every minute. Already it was Thursday. Only eight days remained until Jody's surgery. Only eight days in which to unravel a mystery that reached across a lifetime.

Without Jody the house was empty, lonely. It was barely light outside. While I shaved, I began ticking off the things I must do before beginning the search. Money was an immediate concern. I would have to travel, of course. I had one clue, just one. I knew Jody's birthplace: Fort Wayne, Indiana. This was all the information her adoptive parents had ever given her. Beyond this I knew nothing. Not even a name. What's more, her adoptive parents were dead. They'd taken the secret of her identity with them to the grave.

Where would I start? Obviously, Fort Wayne. But by now Jody's natural parents could be anywhere. So many years had passed. And just because the birth had occurred in Fort Wayne, it didn't necessarily mean they lived there, ever. Her mother could have gone there only for the birth. She could be in California, possibly living right here in Los Angeles. She could be anywhere. And if I found her, would she admit the truth, that she really was Jody's mother? After all, she'd given her baby away. Would guilt keep her silent—even if I found her?

I finished shaving and put a pot of coffee on the stove to heat. Then I placed a telephone call to the city health office in Fort Wayne. Early in my newspaper career I'd been an investigative reporter. Experience told me this was where to begin. I was sure all adoption papers and birth certificates would be on file there.

I was correct.

I explained to the clerk who took the call that I was telephoning from California, that this was an emergency, and that I needed her help.

"What kind of help?" the clerk asked.

"I want my wife's adoption papers and birth certificate," I said.

I might as well have asked for the courthouse dome.

"Adoption records are strictly confidential," the voice said.

"I know, but . . ."

"Strictly confidential."

"But this is an emergency," I pleaded.

I explained about Jody's illness, how only a few days remained to locate her mother.

The voice was implacable. "Those records are sealed. They can't be opened without a court order."

"But my wife—"

"I'm sorry."

It was a voice heavy with the indifference of one who has grown weary dealing in personal tragedies. As a reporter, I'd been bullied before by martinets secure in their world of civil service, dealing with human beings as if they were entries in a ledger. Long ago I'd learned that you don't argue with these people. You sidestep them. I asked to speak with the jurist in charge of adoptions. I was referred to another number.

The woman who answered the phone was courteous. The Judge, she said, was on the bench. Would I care to leave a number? She would give him the message as soon as court recessed.

"Ask him to call me collect . . . please," I said.

When the call finally came, a pleasant voice said, "This is Judge Frank Celarek in Fort Wayne. You called me?"

I repeated my story about Jody. "Judge Celarek," I said, "I have only eight days. . . ."

"Do you have any leads?"

"Only that my wife was born in Fort Wayne."

"Did the adoption take place here?"

"I'm really just guessing, but I believe so," I said.

I gave him the names of Jody's adoptive parents. Perhaps their names would be cross-filed with those of her natural parents, I suggested. Judge Celarek was

not particularly optimistic. Names might not be
enough. After all, my wife was a parent herself now.
We were reaching back across several decades. Births
and even deaths were sometimes not recorded in those
days.

"I've got so little time," I said.

"I understand," he said. He promised that a search
for the records would be started immediately, and
suggested that I call back the next day.

It occurred to me to telephone Natalie Stephenson,
a young Los Angeles woman who advises adoptees
concerning their parental searches.

She was helpful. She suggested I obtain a letter
from Dr. Marxer describing Jody's illness. "Be sure he
indicates this is a medical emergency," she said. "You'll
need all the sympathy you can get."

Early Friday morning I telephoned Judge Celarek
again. The news was distressing. "I'm sorry," he said.
"So far we haven't found a thing."

"Not even a birth certificate?"

"No, not even that."

"Judge, will you keep trying?"

"Yes, certainly. We're going over the records again
right now."

"Just find me one small lead, please. . . ."

Soon I would learn that old adoption records often
are stored in courthouse basements or locked away in
vaults in city health offices. Frequently they are im-
properly indexed, which makes the search frustratingly
difficult. This is particularly true of records processed
prior to World War II, as of course Jody's were.

I called United Air Lines and reserved a seat to Fort

Wayne on a flight Sunday morning. It would be useless
to leave sooner. This was Friday. City offices wouldn't
be open again until Monday.

In the late afternoon I visited Jody at the hospital.
When I told her what I'd been doing, she smiled for
the first time since her nightmare had begun.

"Oh, wouldn't it be wonderful if you could really
find my mother."

I nodded. "I'll try . . . I'll do my best."

Jody's eyes filled with tears. "Jerry, I don't want to
die until I know. . . ."

Judge Celarek telephoned early Saturday morning.

"I've got some news," he said.

"What sort of news?"

"We discovered your wife's last name."

I was stunned. "What is it?"

"Carnahan."

I couldn't help laughing. "Carnahan? Sonofagun,
she's Irish!"

The Judge chuckled. "Sounds like it. Not much, just
a name—but, anyway, let's hope this helps."

I told him I was flying to Fort Wayne the next day.
We agreed to meet at the courthouse Monday morning.

Afterwards I telephoned Jody. When she answered,
I said, "Hello Irish!"

Her voice was weak. "I don't understand."

"You're Irish, honey."

"Irish? Who told you that?"

"The Judge. I just spoke with him. He knows your
last name."

"What is it?"

"Carnahan."

"Carnahan? Are you sure?"

"Positive."

"Carnahan . . ." I could hear her sobbing. And then I heard her repeat the name over and over: "Carnahan, Carnahan . . . Oh, what a lovely, lovely name. . . ."

3

IN THE AFTERNOON JODY WAS WORSE, her vision blurring, her brain reeling. Each time she looked up, black waves swept across the ceiling. Against the wall the clock spun like a top.

I sat by her bed.

She looked up, fragile, terribly pale. "The doctors were here," she whispered.

"I know."

"They think I'm going to die. . . ."

I squeezed her hand. "That's not true," I lied.

"Are you sure, Jerry?"

I argued. "I spoke with Dr. Marxer. He said you'll be fine after the operation."

"Oh, I hope so."

I laughed. "Besides, you've got to get well—remember, I'm the guy who can't even make the toaster work."

She smiled and then closed her eyes—and I thought

of our years together, the persistent mystery that strangely separated us from one another.

I got up and looked out the hospital window. The late afternoon traffic crawled slowly along Santa Monica Boulevard. Five o'clock, I decided, is a lousy time to be traveling anywhere in Los Angeles. That's the hour when they pull the curtain down on the city. Millions of workers begin inching their way back to the suburbs and the homes and gardens that offer temporary solace from the pressures. I looked across the room at my wife, so familiar, so remote, and I wondered: *Who is this woman who has shared my life for so many years?* It was Saturday. I had only until the following Friday to find the answer. Friday was the day of the operation. Six days . . .

I looked at the clock. It was time for our goodbyes.

I kneeled at Jody's bedside and at last she opened her eyes.

I smiled. "Hi, funnyface."

"Hi," she said, her voice a whisper.

"How do you feel?"

"Not so good, Jerry. I don't feel right."

"I know." I paused. "Honey, it's time for me to go."

She looked up. "Please try not to be gone too long."

"I promise," I said.

She smiled. "I hope you find my mother."

"I'll try," I said. "Believe me, Carnahan, I'll try."

I kissed her again, and left before either of us could say any more.

Several hundred miles away, the man everyone called Carny cried out in his sleep. The woman be-

side him nudged him awake, and he sat upright in bed, his face wet with tears.

"Same dream?" the woman asked, switching on the light.

He nodded. "Only this time, Beulah, it was so real . . . it was just like she was here in this room. . . ."

He got out of bed and went into the kitchen, and lit the burner under the coffeepot. It was three o'clock in the morning and a full moon shone through the window of the small house trailer. He was a small man with high cheekbones and brown eyes, and his dark hair was streaked with gray.

Pouring himself a cup of coffee, he recalled the dream again. It was always the same. He had a sister, a beautiful sister, and each time in the dream she'd be standing at the top of a spiral staircase, wearing a long flowing gown, and she'd be calling out to him, "Help me . . ." and he'd run wildly up the stairs, trying desperately to reach her. But the steps would grow higher and steeper and farther apart until, exhausted, he'd drop by the railing. And then he would look up to where she'd been standing and she would be gone. The steps were endless, and she would be gone.

He'd dreamed the same dream ever since his Aunt Betty had told him he had a sister. He was eight years old, and she'd cautioned him not to tell a soul. It was their secret, Aunt Betty said. He mustn't tell anyone. Especially not anyone in his family. But then when he asked her where his sister was, Aunt Betty just shook her head and said, "I'm sorry, I don't know." She knew, though, that he had a sister. She knew that for sure. And so, since then, wherever he went he would always look at faces, hoping . . .

4

SHE WAS SIXTEEN YEARS OLD the day Jody learned that she was adopted. It was a hot summer morning, she remembered, and she and a girl friend were going to the beach. Shortly after eleven o'clock Jody's mother called from the living room.

"Better hurry with your chores, Jody. Ellen's here."

Jody opened the bedroom door. "In a minute... soon as I finish picking up."

Hurriedly she threw some clothes in a hamper. Then she slipped into the new bathing suit her mother had sewn for her out of an old school dress. Although Jody was excited about going to the beach, she was troubled. She'd awakened with an uneasiness she couldn't account for, a mild depression. But why? Studying herself in the mirror she smiled at last, trying to shrug off the blue mood. The new suit fit her tiny figure snugly. She was pleased. With the sun streaming through the window she decided nothing could be wrong. It was much too lovely a day for anything to be wrong.

She picked up her beach towel and hurried into the living room. Ellen Short was tall and bony and undeveloped. Or, more accurately, *underdeveloped*, with red hair and freckles that gave her a boyish appearance. Despite the heat, Ellen wore a sweater over her bathing suit. Everybody agreed that her chest was dismally flat. Several of the boys boasted that even they had bigger boobs.

Jody smiled. "Hi, Ellen."

Ellen got to her feet. "Hi, Jody. Ready to go?"

"Whenever you are."

Jody's mother walked them to the door. "Now don't you get sunburned," she cautioned.

Jody waved. "Don't worry. We've got the umbrella."

Once inside the car, Jody turned excitedly to her girl friend. "Oh, Ellen, wait till you hear!"

"Hear what?" Ellen asked, turning the key in the ignition.

"Allan and I are getting engaged!"

Allan Short was Ellen's brother, and he and Jody had been dating for the last three months.

Ellen reached over and switched off the engine. "When did you decide all this?"

"A couple of days ago."

"Don't you think maybe you'd better wait awhile?" Ellen said.

"Wait? Why?" Jody cried, still smiling.

Ellen looked straight ahead and said, "I'm afraid it won't work."

"What do you mean?"

"I'd just forget it, that's all."

"But why? We've already looked at rings. . . ."

Jody felt the color rising in her face. Why was Ellen acting this way? Other friends were engaged. Maybe some of the couples did break up, but so what? It would be different with Allan. He was steady and good.

Now she heard Ellen saying to her again, "You're just going to have to forget it, Jody."

"But why?"

"Because it simply wouldn't work."

"I don't understand."

"It just wouldn't, that's all."

Jody begged, "Please tell me—"

"I can't."

Jody insisted. "Please."

"I'd rather not."

"Please."

Ellen shrugged. Then, speaking slowly, deliberately, she said, "Because you're adopted. . . ."

It was as if a sledge-hammer had been brought down on her skull. Jody braced herself against the car seat, her heart racing wildly. "Whoever told you anything like that?"

Ellen was staring out the window. "I heard our parents talking about it, yours and mine."

"When?"

"A long time ago. I can't remember when."

"It's not true," Jody cried. "I don't believe you." And then she felt her body begin to shake, her eyes filling with tears. It was not until much later that Jody

remembered hearing something else, something her
friend Ellen had said after she became hysterical.

"Oh, yes, I overheard it," Ellen Short said. "And not
only that you're *adopted*, but that your real parents
weren't even married, either. I mean that makes you,
you know . . . well, illegitimate."

Jody couldn't remember getting out of the car. All
she could remember was running, running away from
Ellen Short, while the sickness rose in her throat. At
one point she turned and cried out, "Don't worry about
your brother . . . I'll never see him again!"

And she never did.

She kept on running. Finally she reached the park,
where she stumbled and fell. She lay on the grass,
face down, for a long time.

When she eventually got to her feet, she had no
idea how long she'd lain there. Her home-made bathing suit was stained by the grass and her head
throbbed. She started toward home. She was in a daze.
The sun flashed off the pavement, bands of heat shim-
mering up from the concrete. She felt lightheaded.
When she reached her own street, she knew she
couldn't face her parents. Not now.

She knocked on a neighbor's door, and began sobbing
again. "Jody, what's wrong?" The woman asked,
alarmed. The neighbor led her into the bathroom,
washed her face, and tried to console her. And when
Jody told her what had happened, the woman made
her promise never to tell her parents.

"It would break their hearts," she said.

Jody never did tell, of course. She kept the secret for nearly thirty years. Both her mother and father died without ever suspecting that Jody had learned—and suffered—the truth so many years earlier.

But all that time, wherever Jody went she studied the faces, searching, praying that someday she'd find one that matched hers. Once at a friend's house in San Francisco Jody saw a man who resembled her. But when she asked if he was from Indiana, he just laughed—he'd never been to Indiana in his life.

Whenever she saw a car with Indiana license plates she'd follow it, hoping that the people in it might know something, might know where her mother lived, or recognize Jody and tell her who her mother was. Often in her dreams Jody would wander into strange towns and try to match the faces with her own, always looking for someone with the same small features, the same dark hair and brown eyes and the pouting mouth. But mostly in these dreams Jody was alone, calling out to a mother who never called back.

Later, after we were married, I would hear her beside me at night, sobbing softly, and I knew what it was. The old nightmare. Everyone had run away and left her alone again. Occasionally she'd dream a happy dream in which her mother held her in her arms and she felt warm and loved and wanted. But when she waked it was always the same, a vague melancholy, a longing.

In Kokomo, Indiana, which is where Jody's adoptive parents lived before moving to California, she would study the faces of strangers whenever she went home for a visit. Sometimes someone would stop her and ask,

"Don't I know you?" and Jody would say, "No, I don't believe so"; but later she would always wonder.

During her childhood, long before Jody learned she was adopted, she envied anyone with brothers and sisters. And whenever she heard them argue she always promised herself that if she had a brother or a sister, someday, they'd never argue. Not ever.

Shortly after her adoptive parents died, she visited a woman her mother had known in Indiana, and the woman confirmed what Ellen Short had told her that sad Sunday years earlier. Yes, she'd been adopted. Her natural mother had been young . . . just a teenager. She came from a small town near Fort Wayne. The name? No, the woman didn't know the name. She only knew that Jody's real mother had never gotten to see her. Jody's adoptive parents had taken her away too soon, right after she was born. The very same day. Jody's mother was pretty, the woman said. At least, that's what Jody's adoptive parents had told her.

Later, the woman said she had heard that the maternity home where Jody was born was gone. It had burned, she explained. All the records were destroyed in the fire. Everything. No use searching. It would be crazy. Besides, Jody's real mother was probably dead. That was a long time ago—oh, my yes, a very long time ago.

But to Jody none of this was in the past—nor would it ever be.

3:30 A.M.
Carny poured himself another cup of coffee. There was no sense in trying to go back to bed now. The

dream about his sister had stirred other memories.
When he was growing up he could never figure out
why he had to live with his grandparents instead of
with his mother, the way other kids did. Carny loved
his mother. He guessed she loved him, too. But he
wasn't allowed to go there much—and he didn't know
why. Only sometimes his grandparents said he could.
This was usually on Saturday. They'd take him to his
mother's house and Carny would play for maybe a
couple of hours with his half brothers. Then his grandparents would always take him back with them again.
And Carny would always get sick when he had to go.
It was always a week before he got to go see his mother
again, and sometimes it was more than that.

Once when he was at his mother's house Carny got
himself into a lot of trouble. He was playing with his
half brothers and he told them Aunt Betty's secret.
About Carny having a sister and all. When his grandparents heard about it, they were really angry, all
right. His granddad gave him a licking.

His grandparents didn't take him there any more.
There were no more Saturdays. His mother wanted
him to come, but Carny's grandfolks said no. It was
shortly after this that his grandfolks moved away from
Auburn to a town called Elwood. It was only about
a hundred miles away. But it seemed a whole lot
farther than that—it seemed to Carny just about as
far away as you could get. He couldn't do anything
about it, though. He had to go where they took him.
They made him go. He guessed he'd never see his
mother again. He was just about twelve years old when
they moved to Elwood. After that Carny got to see
his mother maybe once a year. He tried the best he

could to make believe Saturday came only once a year, but it didn't work. He tried to turn a year into a week, but it just would not come out that way. When you're a kid, you can pretty much always do magic like that. But Carny was twelve now, and when your mother was way over there, and you were here, and no one could do anything about it, then the magic didn't work—then you weren't a kid anymore, no matter how old you were.

5

SHORTLY AFTER NINE A.M., United flight
100 climbed above Los Angeles International and
banked into its flight pattern. I looked down at the
city, the endless grid of streets, houses, yards, cars,
here and there a swimming pool flashing in the morning light.

Let her live, God, please let her come home again....

If nothing else, Jody now knew her nationality,
knew she was Irish. The question had never mattered
to me but it mattered to her. And now I cared because
it mattered so very much to her—this need she had
to fill in the blanks in her life.

"It does something to you," she used to say, "learn-
ing the way I did that you're adopted . . . and then all
those questions start opening all around you."

As the jet continued its steady climb, carrying me
closer to the uncertainty of the future, my thoughts

wandered back over the course of our uncertain marriage—the good times and the bad.

In some ways Jody is childlike, I thought. It's a refreshing innocence others notice and find charming. Even though she's been around newspaper people most of her married life, Jody holds on to that innocence. She's uneasy in crowds, at parties. She doesn't drink. She's shy.

It was a chill December morning in 1941 when I first saw her, a girl on her way to North Hollywood High School, walking along Magnolia Boulevard, all bundled up in a white sweater. I remember I drove by in my vintage Ford and tried to pick her up, but she just smiled shyly. "No, thank you," she said politely, even though the wind was blowing and it was cold. She was small, with a pink ribbon in her hair, and as far as I was concerned she was the prettiest girl I'd ever seen. Every morning for a couple of weeks I offered her a ride. Finally she accepted and we began dating. I think I fell in love with Jody the first time she got into that car. She was different from other girls I'd known. She was quiet and withdrawn, with an innocence that was rare even in the winter of '41. I promised myself that someday I would marry her.

I asked her to a dance right off. It was the only thing I could think of. Only I forgot to mention that I didn't know a single step.

But Jody taught me, and in no time we were going to dances regularly, usually to the Palladium. That was the home of the Big Bands ... Glenn Miller, Tommy Dorsey, Jan Garber. This was our time ... a time of accordion-pleated skirts and bobby sox, sentimental tunes and high school proms. Our hangout was Bailey's Malt Shop in North Hollywood, and the strongest thing we ever drank was a cherry Coke.

"And put in plenty of ice, Mr. Bailey!" we'd yell.

Both of Jody's adoptive parents disapproved of me. Especially her mother. For one thing, Jody's mother wanted Jody just the way she was, childlike. And the same was true of Jody's father. Her folks pretty much agreed on that one score, they thought Jody was the kind of girl who needed a lot of protection, who needed parents, not boyfriends—or a husband. The irony was perfect. Yes, Jody needed parents—more than any of us could have guessed.

The plane pitched and I was jostled out of my reverie. I looked out the window again. We were over the Rockies. I leaned back in the seat and let my thoughts drift back, and saw Jody the first time she ever came over to our house. We lived in a duplex near the Hollywood Bowl, and she rode over on the street-car. When my mother answered the door, well, there was this skinny little kid, eighty-nine pounds of girl called Jody, and she was wearing a white dress and saddle shoes, and she held a bouquet of flowers she'd picked for my mother. Well, everybody in the family fell in love with her right off. Jody overwhelmed my folks just as completely and instantly as she had me.

But Jody's parents just could not get used to me. Especially after they read a letter I'd written to Jody while I was in the Navy. I'd said something that offended them. I don't remember what—but I do remember hearing about how sore they were. They tore up the letter and told Jody she couldn't see me again. Jody was nineteen at the time. So after that I'd drive by at night and blink my lights—and Jody would wave from the window.

Some courtship.

But we managed to see each other often even so. I got my friends to date her. They'd pick Jody up and I'd meet her down the street and we'd go off to the movies or to a dance. Once, though, the system broke down. There was this fellow I didn't trust—so I had him lock me in the trunk of his car. The plan was that he'd go to the door to get Jody while I waited in the trunk. If it sounds crazy, you've forgotten your youth. Anyhow, the guy was a talker, and he was gone so long I damn near suffocated in there.

Eventually Jody's parents gave in and we were married. For our honeymoon we drove to San Francisco. We drove up the coast and stopped to eat in some little town—Half-Moon Bay, I think it was. Only there wasn't a restaurant, just a grocery. So we had jelly rolls and Pepsi-Colas. Some wedding breakfast.

I looked at my watch again. Twelve ten. We'd be landing in Chicago soon. I closed my eyes again.

Our honeymoon was brief. Only three days. I had to get back to a job I had . . . parking cars. I worked across the street from Ken Murray's old "Blackouts," the place where the *Merv Griffin Show* is produced today. The lot was elevated, I remember that, and it overlooked another parking lot just below ours. I could still see myself backing up real fast in an old Packard. Only when I hit the brakes they weren't there. I took off like Superman flying backwards, and landed on top of a car in the lot next door. The boss gave me my check and waved goodbye.

So I enrolled in college, working nights in a body–fender shop and taking classes during the day. When I graduated I got a job on a newspaper, covering every story you can name—kidnappings, robberies, murders. I even reported on the Berlin crisis. Later I got a roving assignment that kept me on the move (still does), traveling around the world to nearly any place you can name. It's the kind of work that left little time for Jody and our two sons. Strange how quickly they'd grown up and gone away, our sons.

In my memory I could still see Dick and Bo as little boys with sunburned noses and dirty faces, doing all the things that little boys do. We spent lazy days swimming and sunning at a favorite cove near Laguna Beach . . . Jody, the boys, and I. We'd go shelling and we'd ride giant waves and we'd feel the sun on our backs. Early in the morning we took long walks along the beach, Dick and Bo skipping rocks along the water and then chasing after sandpipers.

In the late afternoon we'd make the same hike, watching the sun tumble into the sea. During the day we gathered driftwood and at night Jody and I would lie by the fire, counting stars. Down the coast other vacationers spent their evenings in fussy restaurants and crowded bars. But we spent ours chasing grunion and roasting hot dogs and toasting marshmallows.

A couple of summers ago Jody and I tried to recapture the old feeling. But it didn't work out. All we could remember were two little boys with sunburned faces. All those years were gone now, every precious moment. . . .

I heard the stewardess' voice and I opened my eyes. She was announcing our approach to O'Hare. In a short while I would find myself closer to the center of the mystery I sought to unravel. There was so little time. My wife lay dying in Los Angeles, and on Friday a team of surgeons would try to save her life. The outcome would be in God's hands and theirs. In my hands was the single prospect of returning to my wife with a precious gift: her identity.

I had five days to go.

6

WE WERE BARELY OUT of the overcast when the plane touched down in Chicago. The air seemed sticky and uncomfortable as I left the plane. Thunderheads boiled over Lake Michigan. I looked at my watch. Four eleven. My flight to Fort Wayne would depart in less than half an hour.

I walked hurriedly through the terminal. Couples rushed past me, vacationers running to catch their planes. Suddenly I found myself wishing that Jody were here and that we, too, were going somewhere together, that something else lay ahead of us, anything but the uncertainty of Friday.

At the gate marked Fort Wayne I asked for a window seat. I wanted a good first look at Indiana. Later, buckling my seat belt, the courage went out of me. Suddenly the whole effort seemed hopeless, a futile shot in the dark.

For the first time I was overcome by the thought of defeat. What made me think I could find Jody's family? The odds were overwhelmingly against me. And if I failed?

I looked out the window. The plane was high over the great flatlands of Indiana. This was mid-America, with its endless miles of pastures and tall, green corn and soybean fields and rural villages. An afternoon rain had fallen, flooding the deep furrows in the newly ploughed earth. Even from this height I could see that everywhere the land was soggy. It looked as if someone could wring a lake out of the soil. But it had been only a summer squall, and now the black clouds were scrubbed away and the freshly laundered sky was flawlessly blue. The sun flashed off the metal roofs of barns. And beside the barns stood huge silos, casting long shadows across the fields.

Cattle grazed among a network of low, undulating hills far to the right of the plane, the animals black and white and rust-colored against the blazing green of the earth. Beyond, the land flattened out again, and scattered across it were dozens of old farmhouses framed by white rail fences, and by orchards, and by fields of corn that flowed all the way to the horizon.

Would I find her down there, Jody's mother? Was she living in that rambling old home, the one with the gables ... there next to the barn with the tobacco sign on the roof? Or was it that other place down the road, the one set deep in the midst of a brilliant apple-green orchard? Or was Jody's mother huddled away in some tenement in New York—or in some flophouse in Albuquerque?

Below us now were the clustered houses of a rural

town. I studied the churchyard with its row on row of markers. Would my search end here? Was she already dead and buried, Jody's mother? It was a prospect I didn't want to face. I turned from the window as the stewardess announced our arrival. "We will be landing in Fort Wayne shortly. Please be sure your seat belts are fastened securely."

As the green earth came up to meet us, the jet settled gracefully onto a runway lined with military aircraft. Military planes in such a peaceful setting? But wasn't this Fort Wayne—the great American Midwest? I would have other surprises—starting immediately.

I followed the stream of passengers crowding into the small, modern terminal. The lounges and coffee shops were full, and at the far end of the building Hertz and Avis were waiting for the new arrivals.

I passed up their counters. I had no need for a car. Not yet, anyway. I claimed my luggage and waved to a taxi. It was a Checker cab and this surprised me. For some reason I was expecting an old Chevy or a broken-down Ford, something colorfully rural. I had always figured Fort Wayne for a hick town—country music and cow dung—one of those ideas that just sticks in your mind. I had a lot to learn. The driver could see that I was new to town. He rattled off a long list of statistics: the town has a dozen banks, four savings and loan association, several big insurance companies, a couple of newspapers, TV and radio stations, and dozens of diversified firms. And let's not forget that Fort Wayne is Bible Belt country: more than two hundred and thirty churches in town, representing nearly every denomination you can name.

I figured I'd heard enough. "Good speech," I said. "Thanks."

The driver spoke with a decided Midwestern twang. "Hot evenin'," he said. "You sure picked a heck of a time t' come here, mister. Gets muggy this time o' year. Muggier'n all get out."

I studied the evening sky. Once more, dark clouds licked at the horizon. Soon there would be more rain. And after that it would get sticky again.

The cab sped out Ferguson Road and turned toward the city at Brookwood Golf Course, passing mostly old-fashioned, single-story frame houses with tidy yards. Elms grew everywhere. They lined both sides of the road.

"Stays hot all night long durin' summer," the driver continued. "High readings with humidity t' match." He shook his head. "Yessir, stays hot all night. Lots of fireflies. Fireflies and mosquitoes. Sometimes even a tornado touches down."

I pulled off my coat. "But the winters are great, right?"

"Colder'n a cow's hooves! Freeze you right outa business, it will. But you ain't figurin' on stayin' that long, tell the truth."

I said nothing.

On the edge of town we passed several old brick buildings and a couple of industrial plants, grim affairs, like a prison I'd visited once on an assignment.

The driver pointed to a vacant building. "Over there's the Embassy Theater. People 'round here call it the 'Popcorn Palace.' Shut down now, but the city's tryin' t' raise money t' fix 'er up. Used t' be real popular."

Pulling up at the Sheraton, the driver continued his chamber of commerce spiel.

He pointed. "That big ol' outfit yonder with the gold dome's the courthouse."

"Mister," I said, "that's where I aim to spend a lot of time."

"Well, good, son," the driver said, his voice suddenly shrewd, "and I'm tickled t' death t' hear you trying t' talk just like real folks."

We both laughed—and I gave him a bigger tip than I should have.

In my hotel room I phoned Judge Celarek to reconfirm our meeting for eight o'clock the next morning. Then I called Jody.

The nurse said she was sleeping. "Mrs. Hulse had an unsatisfactory day, Mr. Hulse. She was given sedation, and she's resting well now."

I said to tell her that her husband had called. "And, nurse, be sure to tell her I love her. Please, don't forget that." I went into the bathroom and splashed cold water on my face. Then I went down the hall, took the elevator to the bar on the roof, and ordered a Scotch.

"Lots of ice," I said to the bartender, and thought again of the hours we spent at the malt shop when the heart was clear and life seemed forever.

Picture windows lined one wall. I watched the sun sink deep into the flat, wet Indiana soil. The dying rays ignited the three rivers that flow through Fort Wayne: the St. Joseph, the St. Mary's, and the Maumee.

The bartender ran a playback on the cab driver's statistics, then added a few of his own. "Every year," he said, "we get a hundred thousand folks here for the

Three Rivers Parade. Lots of community spirit in this town. Great place in the summertime, too. There's an old riverboat that takes folks crusin' on Shoaff Lake."

"Sounds pleasant," I said, trying to pick up the thread of his monologue.

Suddenly he slapped the bar. "Darn near forgot to mention Johnny Appleseed. That feller's buried right here in Fort Wayne!"

I thought about Los Angeles and the smog and too many people and the violence, and I wondered why anyone ever leaves a place like Fort Wayne for a place like Los Angeles.

Outside now lights were flickering on ... like the fireflies the cab driver had mentioned. In the growing darkness I saw a burned-out building a few blocks away. It was ghostly, the twilight showing through its shell. Someone had told Jody that the home where she was born had burned. Perhaps this was it. But, no, the bartender said it had been an old paint store.

"Lit up the town like the Fourth of July, night she burned," he said.

I spotted the courthouse, its dome lighted in the darkness.

The courthouse: Was Jody's secret hidden somewhere inside, a slip of paper squeezed into a folder and jammed alongside thousands of other files?

I ordered another Scotch and went to bed.

4 A.M.
Carny could see the moon from his trailer window. In his mind's eye he could see another moonlight night

more than thirty years earlier, when he was in a fox-hole in New Guinea and he was thinking of his sister. He might die this night, he knew. There'd been more than a dozen hits in his outfit. Japanese snipers were in the trees, somewhere in the jungle. Every time some-one moved there'd be a burst of gunfire.

Carny looked into the night sky over New Guinea and he prayed. He prayed that he could live through this night and through the rest of the war. He prayed that he would live until he found his sister. Then they started shelling and he forgot what he was praying for and just prayed.

7

IT WAS EIGHT O'CLOCK when I arrived at the courthouse. As I climbed the marble steps I counted the days that remained: four days from now, from this very moment, Jody would be on the operating table. My God, she had so little time . . . we both had so little time.

Inside, the old building had the air of an ancient church, its rotunda filled with a cathedral silence. Sunlight filtered through a magnificent stained glass window set into the dome, so high overhead I had to lean back to see it. My footsteps echoed on the old marble staircase and along the corridor on the upper landing. At the top floor I paused. I was alone, the silence deafening. Perhaps here, somewhere here in this tomblike building, my wife's past lay hidden, yellowing pieces of paper stuck in an old filing cabinet or sealed in a vault. I caught myself praying that this austere place would yield up Jody's secret—her identity.

I opened the door to Judge Celarek's chambers. He was seated behind a desk piled high with notes and legal briefs, a big friendly man in his fifties, large-boned, with gray hair and a kindness that was evident almost immediately.

"Jerry Hulse," I said, offering my hand.

"I'm Frank Celarek," he said, getting to his feet.

He was in his shirt sleeves, and a patch covered one eye. We shook hands.

"Coffee?" he asked. I nodded, and without hesitating he put on his coat and ushered me out the door.

We crossed Calhoun Street and passed a men's haberdashery, a hardware store, and, best of all, people that called out, "Good morning." Fort Wayne is a place where people still care for others; it's an old-fashioned concern that made America special once. On Berry Street we turned into a cafe with a garish sign and tables with Formica tops. A fan spun over-head and a fly buzzed inside the glass candy case next to the cash register.

We took a table near the window. While we sipped our coffee, Judge Celarek told me about growing up in Fort Wayne. His people were Polish immigrants, and he'd worked his way through Butler University and Indiana Law School by washing dishes and sweeping floors. His home was Fort Wayne, and he belonged to the Elks and the Eagles and the Moose and the Knights of Columbus, and even belonged to an old-timers' softball team. While he was telling me this, the waitress poured our coffee.

"Mornin', Judge."

"Good morning, Millie."

"Having breakfast?"

"No, just coffee." He looked up. "How about you, Jerry?"

I shook my head. "Coffee's fine."

The Judge stirred a spoonful of sugar into his coffee, and got down to it. "How long have you and Jody been married?" he asked.

I thought for a minute. "Let's see. Twenty-eight years next October."

"Quite a spell," the Judge said.

"We were just kids," I said. "As a matter of fact, you won't believe this, but Jody actually sold her *bike* to raise the cash to buy me a wedding gift."

"It's been a good marriage then?"

"In a way . . ."

The Judge was silent, and so was I—and then I said, "It's had its share of problems, I guess. For one, her parents, especially her mother."

"Oh . . ."

"She was jealous, resentful, could never let go of her daughter, and Jody was always trying so damn hard to please her parents. I guess she felt she owed them something because they adopted her."

"I can understand that," Judge Celarek said, nodding to an older man who passed the table.

I shrugged. "I suppose. But it was strange . . . I mean, I hadn't married Jody, I'd entered into a contract with her parents. In a way I was sort of working as a caretaker to their daughter. And, finally, when they died Jody needed me. But it was strange because it was for the first time."

The Judge pushed his cup to one side. "They didn't know Jody knew she was adopted?"

"Jody never told them."

"And they're both dead?"

I nodded. "She still broods about not having an identity. . . ."

The waitress shuffled toward our table, holding a steaming pot. "More coffee?"

I shook my head.

The Judge pushed his cup forward. "I'll have a refill, Millie."

When she was gone I said, "Several years ago I cleared out. I needed time to think things over. . . ."

He lit his pipe. "Oh, is that so?"

"It didn't work, really. All I found out was how much I really loved Jody . . . and how lousy it was that it never seemed enough."

"So you moved back?"

I nodded.

"Were things any better?"

"No, there was still that gap, this thing that's missing in her life—in both our lives."

"The . . . uh, identity?"

"Judge Celarek, I don't believe that Jody or our marriage can ever be complete until she knows."

"And now, because of this crisis—for you it's also a crisis in your marriage."

"That's exactly it," I said, looking down at the table.

"I have four days to make it right, to fill in those empty spaces."

He lit his pipe again and pushed his chair away from the table. He was standing now. "If she lives, Jerry, if she lives, you'll have lots of time to make it right."

"And if she doesn't. . . ?"

The Judge motioned. "Come on, let's get back to the courthouse."

8

THE SEDATIVE HAD WORN OFF and Jody
was awake, the dream still vividly with her. It was
about her adoptive parents, she told me later on the
phone, a dream that swept her back once more into
that grim house of her youth. Her mother's love had
been overpowering, demanding, destructive—an all-
consuming love, uncontrolled in its hunger. Jody's
father couldn't cope with it, and so he spent longer
hours in the taverns. At last, in a frantic effort to save
their marriage, Jody's mother had decided to adopt a
baby. She would bring her husband securely into the
home again, the baby would bring him back, the baby
would be her ticket to happiness. And so on May 13,
1925, Jody was "born" into that unhappy household.

But the stratagem failed, for Bruce Carr, Jody's
father, continued to drink and to seek other com-
panionship. Jody remembered especially the night-

mare of her thirteenth birthday and her party. Her mother had prepared Jody's favorite, chicken and dumplings, and there was a cake with thirteen candles. As Jody blew out all the candles her friends sang "Happy Birthday," and then they gathered in a circle while she opened the gifts. First there was a new wastebasket from her parents, Bruce and May Carr. This was for her room. As she opened the other gifts, she placed each one inside the wastebasket. She was especially fond of the gold crucifix a girl named Barbara had given her.

Finally, with everything unwrapped, the girls sang "Happy Birthday" again. The chorus was just ending when Jody heard a loud pounding on the door. Her mother got up to answer it. "You stay with your friends," May Carr told her daughter. "I'll see who it is."

When Mrs. Carr opened the door, Bruce Carr stumbled in. Drunk, he staggered on into the living room. May Carr called after him, "Bruce, for Heaven's sake, it's the child's birthday—"

The man turned, nearly fell, and muttered, "So what?"

Stunned, embarrassed, Jody's friends prepared to leave. But the man weaved back across the room— toward the new wastebasket. Jody watched, paralyzed. He teetered and nearly fell again. Jody cried for him to stop. "Please," she begged. He reeled above the wastebasket. And then, suddenly, he was kneeling, the man was sick, terribly sick. The party guests stood transfixed. The silence was colossal—a quiet that was unimaginable, until there came the spasms of a grown man retching.

The party was over.

Bruce and May Carr were married in Kokomo, Indiana, a dozen years before they adopted Jody. May Carr was the daughter of a Christian minister, and Bruce Carr was a lumberman's son. He was a dashing and handsome man; she was blue-eyed and beautiful —and they were deeply in love. At one point they enrolled together in Bible school, deciding to become evangelists. But it didn't take Bruce Carr long to learn he had no serious calling for the gospel. Abandoning the pulpit for other pursuits, he became in succession a theater operator, a haberdasher, a gambler, a bootlegger, cab driver, cook, and years later, when he'd given up the bottle, a respected employee of a California aircraft company.

But there was little harmony in the Carr home no matter what the status of Bruce Carr. Jody recalled to me the dreadful tension, the expectation of terrible confrontations that dogged all their days. May Carr was domineering. Bruce Carr was generally passive— or else he wasn't there at all. Jody was forced into the role of appeaser, the pawn in this intolerable conflict. Because of her mother's powerful and persuasive personality, Jody felt inferior. Neither of her parents recognized her sensitivity. Nor did they realize how the constant wrangling assaulted Jody's precarious emotions. Her school grades suffered while she groped her way through a childhood of deepening depression and discord.

But Jody never questioned her parents' love for her. It was genuine enough—this she knew. And it was huge. But it was also selfish, absolutely possessive, a prod continually reminding Jody of the price they paid for her: this hateful, pitiless marriage that was sustained on her behalf. In the end, Jody's feelings of guilt were as huge as the love that was offered her. She became a gloomy child, a child increasingly turned inward toward the dark drama unfolding in her heart.

There had been one particularly bitter fight—when Jody's mother, as usual, was nagging her father, who was, as usual, drinking. A terrible battle ended with his driving off with Jody to a poker parlor downtown. Somehow he found a crib for her there, and then he played cards and continued to drink. Jody remembered watching the roomful of strangers through the bars of the crib. Only a single dim light bulb lit the spectacle before her, cigar and cigarette smoke rolling through it like a noxious mist boiling up from the earth. She remembered looking up at the figures, motionless, shadowy. When she complained that she was thirsty, Bruce Carr brought her a Coca-Cola, and then went back to his cards. Later she remembered sunlight sweeping away the darkness, and him driving her home. It was dawn when he deposited her on the sidewalk in front of the house and sped away.

Jody was five years old.

These were the Depression years and Bruce Carr was frequently unemployed, and so he baby-sat while May Carr worked. Only instead of caring for Jody at home, he took her someplace else—to a woman's apartment. Jody could still recall the musty smell and the wretched iron bed in the room where Bruce Carr and the woman locked her. The shades were drawn and she'd lie in the dark, terrified. Once she cried out to her father, and when he didn't answer she called again, hysterical this time. Finally Bruce Carr shouted back, "Shut up!"

Later, when Bruce Carr quit drinking, Jody became his constant concern. As she grew older, he tried desperately to create new images in an effort to wipe out the old. He bought her a used bicycle, which he painted and polished until it shone like new. And then he grew extravagantly suspicious of every boy Jody dated. At the same time, her mother cautioned her repeatedly, "Don't get serious."

Although nearly an adult now, Jody was treated like a child, forbidden to go ice-skating or roller-skating or to parties with other girls her own age. Increasingly she was protected, confined, smothered, blocked in all her efforts to grow into a woman. When she wanted to get a job she was told nice girls didn't work. And the idea that one day she might marry was never even discussed. Indeed, Bruce and May Carr let it be understood that marriage was in no way a prospect to be contemplated. It did not exist.

The ultimate affront occurred one Saturday while she was at the movies and her parents found, read, and destroyed her letters. Bitter as she was, tempted as she was, Jody did not strike back, did not confront them with the dreadful knowledge that she had, this *immensity* that the fact of her adoption had become.

She kept her secret, putting it behind her back, a club she would not use. For with all the unhappiness, she loved them too greatly ever to hurt them, even slightly.

Some of the saddest moments she remembered were when her parents operated a small restaurant in downtown Los Angeles. The customers sat at a dozen stools lining the long counter. While Jody washed dishes (and her father drank and cooked), her mother would exchange jokes with the customers. It was something Jody always resented, the off-color jokes. Even now she could recall the vulgar laughter, the greasy hamburgers, the foul cigarette smoke, the smell of alcohol on the breath.

Finally Bruce Carr stopped drinking—after the doctor warned him to give it up or die—and the Carrs bought a home in the San Fernando Valley. Miraculously, their marriage had hung together, and these final years were their happiest, a brief interval of peace. But when Bruce Carr died in 1961, May Carr lost all interest in living. Despite the infidelity, the arguments, and the drinking, she had loved him, always, as few women ever love a man. He was her reason for wanting a child in the first place.

Shortly after Bruce died, May suffered a stroke. Three years later she too was dead.

Still, Jody could remember an occasional bright moment from her childhood. She adored her Aunt Verd and she loved to visit her Aunt Helene, both maternal aunts. Aunt Helene drove a Rolls Royce, sailed a yacht, lived in a mansion in Beverly Hills. When Jody visited there she could soak in a bubble bath, stay up till midnight, even have her breakfast in bed.

Aunt Helene was Helene Clark Inman Reynolds Mills de la Torres, and the reason for all the names was that she'd married so many men, among them Walter Inman, the millionaire half brother of tobacco heiress Doris Duke. Husband number one, by the way, had been songwriter Grant ("Ragtime Cowboy Joe") Clark.

Aunt Helene moved in a wacky world of booze, boyfriends, and big bank accounts. Once in a New York night club she startled everyone by staging an impromptu striptease on a table.

Another time, after a particularly late night, Aunt Helene had called down to the maid and asked, "What in the world are all the books doing soaked?" and the maid had shouted back, "That's what we was wonderin' last night, ma'am, when you decided to water the library with the garden hose!"

She was gorgeous, Jody remembered, an absolutely stunning creature who had a home full of friends, food, liquor, and who herself was full of fun. Jody had a glimpse of another world.

4:15 A.M.
No one ever celebrated Carny's birthday. It had always been a hush-hush thing. His grandparents always ignored it. They acted as if it were just another day. Carny knew what birthdays are supposed to be like, but he never said a word. Once, when one of the neigh-

bor kids asked, "Hey, Carny, how come you never have a birthday?" Carny ran off and hid in a field and did a lot of crying.

It worried him at school, because whenever it was somebody's birthday there'd be a party, and Carny was always afraid that the teacher would ask him about his. She never did, though. What with so many kids, he figured she just forgot.

Once, though, a neighbor lady baked Carny a cake, a big chocolate beauty with eleven candles on it. He remembered how he ate till he thought he'd burst. But that was the only time anyone noticed it was his birthday.

It was like that on Christmas too. There wasn't much fuss. At Grandma's they never put up a tree. But once he got to help Aunt Betty decorate hers. It was a toy tree, and she let him put on the tinsel.

At Grandma's there'd be a Christmas dinner, and sometimes Carny would get a new shirt or maybe a pair of socks. But nobody ever told him to hang up his stocking, because Santa Claus just wasn't mentioned in that house. He remembered how one Christmas, when he was fourteen, a school friend gave him a new sweater. Another time Grandma gave him a xylophone, only he didn't get to keep it long. Christmas wasn't even over and she took it away. Carny was making too much noise, she said.

That was always the time when Carny missed his mother most . . . on Christmas Day.

9

JUDGE CELAREK was on the telephone. He was backtracking, speaking with everyone he'd called earlier. They gave him the same message, and it was not the one he wanted to hear. There was nothing new.

All we knew for sure was that last name, Carnahan. I'd already called every Carnahan in the Fort Wayne telephone directory the night before. There were seven. I'd drawn seven blanks.

The Board of Health was still trying to determine the mother's first name and home town, Frank Celarek said. One cause of confusion was the birth certificate. It had been hand written by the attending physician— and it was illegible. To make matters worse, the document was badly faded. And, incredibly, the same was true of the adoption papers—the information on these yellowed pages was also illegible.

There was simply nothing new about Jody's mother,

the judge said, his face already showing his own discouragement.

Still, his inquiries had produced other information. He had learned that the attorney who drew up the adoption papers was deceased. He'd died years ago. He also knew the names of the doctor who had delivered Jody and the woman who operated the maternity home where Jody was born. I jotted them down.

I was still curious about the maternity home. It was a long shot, but I figured it would be worth checking. I studied the name of the woman who had operated it: Annie MacDougall. And the name of the physician who had delivered Jody: Dr. A. E. Edwards.

Meanwhile, Judge Celarek carefully read Dr. Marxer's letter describing Jody's illness: "Patient has extracranial vascular disease . . . strong genetic factor . . . cause of death in either parent would be significant . . . patient's desire to learn her identity important . . . could affect will to survive the operation."

Then he telephoned the Board of Health again. He told the woman who answered to continue checking Jody's file. Perhaps she could decipher the mother's first name and the home town. He emphasized the urgency.

It was time I got going on some investigating of my own. For one thing, I wanted to check the local newspapers. Maybe a notice of Jody's birth had been entered among the vital records . . . the birth of a female child to a woman named Carnahan.

Judge Celarek walked me to the door.

Only a few stragglers remained on the street. Everyone else was inside trying to stay cool. I felt a sudden blast of hot air. The summer wind scattered papers along the street. I looked down. Flowers were wilting in a box beside the courthouse. I could feel the pavement burning through the soles of my shoes. As I stood on the corner, another blistering breeze funneled its way down Main Street. And then it was quiet. Quiet and terribly hot. It was one of those days when the drone of a bee cuts through the stillness like the whine of a jet.

There are two newspapers in Fort Wayne: the *Journal-Gazette* and the *News-Sentinel*. Both occupy the same building. It was too hot to walk even one block. I saw a cab parked across the street and waved to the driver. He burned rubber swinging a U-turn.

"Where to?" he asked.

"The *Journal-Gazette*."

Four blocks later we pulled up in front of a modern, two-story building. "This is it," he said, disappointed at the short hop.

I got out. "Keep the meter running, I'll be back," I told him, and I guess that raised his spirits some.

Inside, I asked to see the old birth notices, specifying month and year. The librarian shoved a huge file across the counter. I began leafing through dozens of yellowed clippings. There were Collinses and Cunninghams and Curtises and bunches of others. But no Carnahans. I went over them again, carefully. Nothing.

Then I walked through the building to the *News-Sentinel*, where a reporter said the librarian was on her lunch hour. I repeated my story about Jody and told him I worked for the *Los Angeles Times*. Reporters, like cops, are clannish. He offered to help.

He opened a file cabinet and dragged out several fat envelopes stuffed with old birth notices. He scattered

them across a table. We divided them up, and together we began checking. Finally we gave up. There
was nothing. Again, not a single Carnahan.

The young reporter looked at me. "Sorry," he said.

I shrugged. "So am I."

Outside, the cabbie was still waiting.

"City library," I told the driver.

The genealogy department is at the far end of a
hallway on the second floor of the library. The room
was crowded, visitors seated at long tables, thumbing
through huge volumes for bits of information relating
to their ancestry.

I spoke with two library assistants, Ila Gruse and
Gerry Pilotte, explained about the urgency of my
search, and they volunteered to help.

"The adoption records," I said, "let me see them,
please."

Miss Pilotte was apologetic. "But we don't keep
adoption papers. Just copies of birth and death
certificates."

Birth certificates.

Maybe I was getting somewhere. I asked Miss
Pilotte if I could see Jody's, writing out the name
Carnahan for her.

"When was she born?" Miss Pilotte asked.

I gave her the date. Right away I could tell something was wrong.

"I'm sorry," she said. "The birth records here don't
go back that far. You'll have to try the Board of Health
for anything like that."

She offered to call the Board for me. I told her not
to bother, that Judge Celarek had already been in

touch with them. I gave her the names of the doctor and the woman who ran the maternity home. "Maybe there's something in your files," I said desperately. "I don't know what exactly . . . but *something*."

Miss Pilotte wanted to know if they had lived in Fort Wayne. I told her yes, years ago. It would take perhaps a half-hour to check, she said. I told her I'd be downstairs in the microfilm department. I wanted to look through old issues of the Fort Wayne newspapers. Maybe I could still find the birth notice.

Already I'd used up most of a day. This left only three. . . .

A librarian brought me two reels of film. I threaded one into the viewer and cranked it forward to May 13, the day of Jody's birth. For the next half-hour I sat fascinated, winding the microfilm through, reading page after page about the world . . . on the day that my wife was born.

The weather report indicated it had been a chilly day, a frost causing widespread damage to Fort Wayne's fruit and vegetable crops. A warming trend was forecast, though, with the temperature going up to 60 degrees. I checked the stock market. Everyone was making money, it seemed. On the front page, a story about Abby Rockefeller told of her plans to marry a twenty-five-year-old attorney. Only she was asking that the word "obey" be omitted from the vows. Women's Lib, as far back as *that*, I couldn't help thinking.

I read Jody's horoscope. It gave promise of an "auspicious life." Just what did *that* mean?

I kept cranking the film through the viewer, searching page by page for an item naming a new mother called Carnahan. There was nothing for May 13. I cranked it ahead to the May 14 issue. Still nothing. I read through the entire month of May. Nothing.

It seemed that Jody had come into this world entirely unnoticed.

The newspaper had devoted copious space to deaths as well as to society notes. A "Miss Virginia Gilton" and a "Miss Ruth Fry" had visited Chicago, and "William Leggett" had motored to New York to vacation with friends.

Dammit, I thought, didn't anyone care about a little girl who was born this day? Wasn't a new life worth a paragraph . . . a single line?

I was rewinding the film when Miss Pilotte hurried down the stairs clutching something in her hand.

"Here," she said, "I think you'll want to read this."

It was a photostatic copy of a story from the front page of the *News-Sentinel*, dated January 2, 1938, and it told about the doctor I was searching for: "Dr. A. E. Edwards, aged fifty-eight, for thirty years a practicing physician and surgeon, committed suicide today by drinking carbolic acid in his office. He died at 10 o'clock while being taken to Lutheran Hospital. A verdict of suicide was returned by Dr. Raymond J. Berghoff, Allen County Coroner. He believed that Dr. Edwards drank the poison about an hour before he was found unconscious by his secretary. He left no note."

The story went on to say that Edwards had been in poor health, who his next of kin were, and so forth.

Miss Pilotte looked at me. "Darn shame," she said.

"That's the way it's been going," I said. "You learn anything about Mrs. MacDougall?"

Miss Pilotte shook her head: she'd searched through several directories, but no mention of the maternity home.

I handed her my card. "I'm at the Sheraton," I said. "If you find something, please call me right away."

On the way back to the hotel I stopped by the Department of Public Welfare. Perhaps Jody's mother had requested financial aid. It was only a hunch, but I had to play every one. Maybe the D.P.W. would have a record. The receptionist introduced me to a Miss Ellwood, a young and pretty woman who listened sympathetically to my story and then led me into her office.

"Wait here," she said, "I'll see what I can find in the basement. We have stacks of old files down there."

As she disappeared down a back stairway, I got the sense of a grim scavenger hunt for Jody's past, bits and fragments stored in basements all over town, an old jigsaw puzzle with the key pieces missing. I'd scrambled around, done a full day's digging—met with Judge Celarek, checked the newspapers, been to the library. I had failed to find the birth notice, and the doctor I had hoped to see was dead, a suicide. I had come up with exactly nothing.

I looked around Miss Ellwood's office. It was cheerless, a dull expanse of gray walls unrelieved by a window or even a picture—nearly as bare and empty, I decided, as my file on Jody.

I was still gazing at the gray walls when Miss Ellwood returned, her expression telling me that she'd found nothing.

"I'm really very sorry," she said. "I looked in every conceivable place. . . ."

I got up to go. "Thanks," I said. "It was kind of you."

She smiled. "Don't give up."

"I'll stay with it, don't you worry," I said, and I left. Back at the Sheraton, I telephoned Judge Celarek. It was five o'clock.

"How'd your day go?" he asked.

"Dead ends."

"That's too bad. Nothing new here either." He paused. "But they're still trying over at the Board of Health."

He told me to telephone again in the morning. I hung up and asked the operator to get me Room 386 at St. John's Hospital in Los Angeles. Jody answered, her voice noticeably weaker. "Where are you?" she asked.

"Still in Fort Wayne."

"How is it?"

"Hot, really hot, but it's a nice town. Nice people."

"I'd like to go there some day."

"You will," I promised, "you will."

And then she said what I didn't want to hear: "Have you found out anything yet . . . about my mother?"

I had to lie. "I've got a few leads, honey. I'm making some headway. The Judge believes the people at the Board of Health might have something soon. We'll find your family. I promise."

"I miss you."

"I miss you, too, Little Jo, I miss you, too."

I hung up. It would be dark soon. Monday evening. And I had to fly out Thursday morning to be with Jody before she had the operation. This meant hardly more than two working days left.

I looked out the window, into the gathering darkness, asking myself, *"Where are you, Mrs. Carnahan. . . ?"*

5:00 A.M.

Carny couldn't recall many happy days growing up. There was one, though, that was special. He was still living in Auburn and his grandpa took him to the company picnic. His grandpa had a farm, but he also worked for the Auburn Automobile Company, and they were putting on this picnic.

A neighbor boy came along, and everyone had the grandest time. Carny was given an entire envelope full of tickets. They were good for all the rides and all the hot dogs and all the soda pop he could eat and drink.

Just this once he got to do all the things other kids got to do. He got to ride ponies and roller-skate, and there was a miniature train. The picnic was held at a lake, and he slid down a slide into the water. He and Grandpa and Grandma and the neighbor boy stayed the entire day, clear till four o'clock in the afternoon. A band played and there were balloons. And Grandpa got a twenty-year pin from the Auburn Automobile Company, and everybody applauded when they gave it to him, and Carny had the best time of his life that day, and he got an idea of what it was like, what it was really like, to be a kid.

10

ON TUESDAY MORNING Judge Celarek had nothing new to report. The Board of Health was still working on it, still trying to locate other records. I agreed to call him later in the afternoon.

The name Annie MacDougall still stuck in my mind. I picked up the telephone directory. There were a couple of MacDougalls listed. I dialed the first one. It was busy. I didn't bother to wait. I called the second number. A woman answered. I told her I was looking for Annie MacDougall.

"She used to operate a maternity home here," I said. "This was years ago."

"Why, you must be talking about my mother-in-law," the voice said.

The long shot!

Anxiously, I asked to speak with Mrs. MacDougall.

"Oh, goodness," the voice said, "she's been dead for years. . . ."

So the friends of Jody's adoptive family had been correct. Mrs. MacDougall was indeed deceased.

"I understand the maternity home she ran was destroyed in a fire," I said.

There was a quick laugh. "Oh, my, *no*. Least it was still standing the last time I was by there."

Was I onto something?

"Were there any records?" I asked.

"Records?"

"Of the babies born there."

I explained about Jody and told her that this was an emergency.

"Oh, I'm *sorry*," the voice said. "I don't know anything about any *records*."

"Is there someone who might know?"

A pause. "Well, there's a man lives there in that old house. Maybe he could help."

She gave me the man's name and the address of the maternity home. I thanked her hurriedly and rushed downstairs to the lobby. There was a cab at the entrance. I pushed a slip of paper with the address into the driver's hand and got in.

It had rained during the night. The air was wet and heavy, and the moisture was being sucked up by a hot sun. I rolled down a window and pulled off my jacket. The leather seat was damp.

Bit by bit, I was beginning to piece together the mystery, speaking with the living, reaching out to the dead. It was a nerve-racking game, yet for the first time I was beginning to feel hopeful. But was it all happening fast enough? With only forty-eight hours until my homeward flight, was this thing going to come together in time?

Ten minutes away from the hotel, the cab stopped before an enormous old mansion.

I asked the driver to wait. Outside the entrance, I gazed up at the Victorian colossus, its façade laced with gingerbread. A row of gables cast shadows down onto the yard. I noticed someone, half-hidden, watching from a window on the second floor.

Even in the noon heat I felt a chill.

I knocked on the door. There was no answer. I knocked again. Finally I walked around to the side of the house and rang another doorbell. Trucks rattled by. Perhaps whoever was inside couldn't hear above the racket. I pushed the bell again. And then the door suddenly opened. It was the man I'd seen peering from the window.

"Sorry to keep you waiting," he said. "I was busy upstairs moving furniture."

His shoes were scuffed, and a gold chain hung at his paunch.

I introduced myself and told him about speaking with the woman on the phone.

We shook hands. "Name's Watkins," he said. "What can I do for you?"

"My wife," I said. "She was born here—"

He interrupted. "Mister, lots of babies were born in this here house. This here was the MacDougall Maternity Home."

I stepped closer. "How long has it been closed?" I asked.

Watkins sighed. "Oh, years now—years. Mrs. Mac-Dougall's been gone since, oh, 1954. Mother Mac died in her eighty-seventh year."

Watkins led me into the living room and handed me

an old newspaper clipping. It was Mrs. MacDougall's obituary. I sat down in a high-backed rocker and began reading. She'd been a member of the Daughters of the American Revolution . . . the Fort Wayne Chamber of Commerce . . . the American Cancer Society . . . Fort Wayne Baptist Church.

Watkins bowed his head. "When she died she was the Church's oldest parishioner."

He handed me a picture. "That was Mother Mac," he said solemnly.

It was the photo of a white-haired woman wearing rimless glasses, a woman who looked very like the one on See's candy boxes. She was holding an infant in her arms.

Watkins looked up at the ceiling. "I've never known a living soul like Mother Mac." He shook his head sadly. "The kindest creature who ever lived. Helped others all her life. By golly, just amazing how Mother Mac cared for those babies, sometimes be up all night long with the little tykes."

Had she ever held Jody? I wondered.

Watkins himself had worked for Mrs. MacDougall. When she died he bought the old mansion from her estate.

I handed back the newspaper clipping. "Mr. Watkins," I said, "could I see the room where my wife was born?"

"The maternity room? Why, yes—yes, of course."

He seemed pleased that anyone would be curious about the old home. He led me through the kitchen again and up a circular stairway to the second floor. The house was ominously silent. Halfway down a hall, he stopped before an open door and pointed. "This here was the maternity room."

I stood in the doorway. A single light hung from the ceiling, and there was a heater against one wall. Otherwise the room was bare, barren, eerily empty of any sign of life.

Watkins opened a closet. "Medical supplies was kept in here," he said.

The sun shone through the window and birds were singing, and yet I felt a deep melancholy, a sudden aloneness, standing in this room where Jody was born. And the mother? Was it night or daytime when she felt the first labor pains? What were her thoughts when she heard her infant daughter cry? It was here, in this place, that mother and daughter were separated. Forever? Strangers had come and taken a child from its mother. Forever?

The old man stepped back into the hallway. "Anything else you'd like to see?"

I followed him. "Why, yes, the records if you don't mind."

He looked at me curiously. "Records. . . ?"

"Yes, of the babies who were born here."

He shook his head. "Weren't no records," he said. "None at all."

His tone was final. I looked around the room one last time. The emptiness was overpowering.

The old man led the way back down the stairway. Outside on the porch I tried again. "Mr. Watkins, would anyone else know about the records?"

He shook his head. "No, 'fraid not. I guess you're just plumb out of luck."

I thanked him for his kindness and got back in the cab. The old man watched from the porch. "Good luck," he called out.

Then the taxi turned the corner and the old gabled mansion disappeared behind us.

I looked at my watch. One o'clock. I told the driver to drop me at the city library.

The library was crowded. I asked to see the old telephone directories. I waited while an attendant rolled several volumes out on a cart. Curious, she asked what I was looking for. When I told her, she volunteered to help. But this was something I wanted to do alone; I didn't want to risk overlooking even a single name. And what I was looking for was the name Carnahan.

I took a legal pad out of my briefcase and began jotting down numbers as I thumbed through the old directories. The pages were fragile. Several were missing. I turned them carefully, one by one. I was concentrating on the years just before and after Jody's birth. Finally I had five names. Another long shot, but I was working ever closer against the clock. Only one more day. Maybe one of these Carnahans was the one I was looking for.

Now I asked for the death records. Perhaps a relative of a late Carnahan would remember a woman who'd given her infant daughter away. The deceased's address would be on the death certificate. Someone somewhere had to remember. . . .

This time I accepted the librarian's offer of help. While not everyone has a telephone, eventually we all die, and so there were hundreds of names. Fortunately they were listed alphabetically. We spent nearly two hours checking. When we'd finished, it was nearly five o'clock. I hurried back to the hotel and called Judge Celarek.

He sounded weary. "Been playing every reasonable hunch, but still nothing," he said. "We're not giving up, though."

We agreed to meet for breakfast at the same place.

I showered and changed clothes and went downstairs. At the hotel entrance I saw the driver who'd picked me up at the airport on Sunday. He waved and I went out onto the sidewalk.

"You still here?" he said, smiling.

"Mind if I sit up front?" I asked.

"No. Where d'you want t' go?"

I showed him my list and he frowned. "All those places?"

"All of them," I said.

"Ooo-eee, that'll take all evenin'."

"It might even take until tomorrow morning," I said. "Let's just get going."

"Where you want t' start?" he asked.

I handed him the list. "It's your town, you figure it out."

"Might as well get goin' with that one," he said, pointing to an address near the bottom. "It's closest."

He gunned the cab up a side street, swung a left onto Calhoun, and kept driving until we got to an old tenement building at the far end of town.

"This it?" I asked.

He nodded.

I got out and walked up to the door. I was about to knock when I saw the sign: NO TRESPASSING—THIS BUILDING HAS BEEN CONDEMNED.

Back in the cab, I said, "Okay, pick another one."

He turned toward the airport. We'd gone a couple of miles out of town when he pulled into the driveway of an attractive two-story brick home.

I rang the bell and a woman answered.

"I'm looking for people named Carnahan," I said.

She was puzzled. "Carnahan?"

"Yes, they lived here once, I believe."

She shook her head. "I'm afraid you have the wrong address. There's no one here by that name." She slammed the door.

We tried another address. Then another and another. I checked my watch. Nine o'clock. I hadn't eaten since breakfast. I spotted a MacDonald's ahead.

"Pull in there," I told the driver. "I'll buy us dinner."

"You sure runnin' up a heck of a bill," he said. By now the meter read $18.80.

We ordered and then the cabbie looked at me curiously. "None of my business," he said, "but what the hell y' huntin?"

I didn't want to talk about it anymore, so I just said the first thing that popped into my head. "I'm looking for my wife," I said. "She's lost."

"Jeez," the driver said, "that's rough, mister."

Back in the taxi, we searched until nearly midnight before we'd exhausted the list. We'd found vacant lots, office buildings, deserted homes . . . and two Carnahans. But neither Carnahan knew anything about the Carnahan I wanted to know about.

The meter read $35.20 when we got back to the hotel. I handed over two $20 bills and got out of the taxi, but the cabbie honked and reached across the seat, pushing one of the bills back into my hand.

"What's this?" I asked.

"Just a little Hoosier hospitality," he shouted, and shoved the taxi into gear and sped away.

11

I met with Judge Celarek the next morning at the cafe on Berry Street. The same waitress brought us coffee.

"You look tired," the judge said.

I shrugged. "Yesterday was a long one."

I told him about finding the maternity home, about going to the library, about the long search in the taxi, about all of my frantic efforts.

The Judge studied my face. "Now what?" he said.

"I don't know." I shook my head. "I don't really know."

"You're going home tomorrow?"

"I've got to. The operation is day after...."

We strolled back to the courthouse. Outside, I looked up at the old building and cursed it silently. Somewhere inside its walls the secret still lay hidden.

We climbed the marble stairs to the Judge's chambers and he unlocked the door.

"Come in," he said. "Court doesn't convene for half an hour yet. We can visit for a bit."

I sat facing him from across his desk, still piled high with papers, things he probably should have been doing instead of backstopping me. Had it been only two days since we'd met? It seemed longer. I had the feeling I'd known Frank Celarek a lifetime. I knew he was a friend, that I could count on him whatever might happen.

He started opening his mail. "More coffee?" he asked.

I shook my head.

He swiveled in his chair and stared solemnly out the window. "I'm sorry," he said. "We came close." Then he turned and lit his pipe, his gaze fixed intently on me.

I looked down at his desk. "I think she could face death ... if she knew for sure who she was...." Absently, I began thumbing through Jody's file, studying the notes and documents I had gathered before leaving Los Angeles.

Now I saw something I hadn't noticed before. It was a number on Jody's birth certificate—not the sealed document the Judge had said was illegible, but the amended birth certificate that named only the adoptive parents.

"Do you suppose this means anything?" I said, pointing to the number.

Judge Celarek looked at it, studied it carefully, and then he picked up the telephone. It's crazy, I know, but I have no idea who it was he called. I never did ask. And Frank Celarek never told me. Evidently the

number on the amended birth certificate referred to
another file with additional background on Jody's
adoption. All I know is that later, when the call was
returned, Frank Celarek was grinning like a bear. He
didn't say anything; he just grinned and handed me a
slip of paper that he'd written something on. It was a
name. It was Edith. It was Edith Carnahan.

"Is there a town?" I asked.

"She's from a little place about forty miles from
here," he said. "Town called Auburn."

I sat dumbfounded. Then I was on my feet and starting out the door. I paused, my hand on the doorknob.
"Judge, I . . ."

He smiled. "Go on, boy, beat it on out there."

"I'll call you," I said.

I took the stairs two at a time and ran out onto
Calhoun Street. I crossed Berry against a signal and
kept right on running . . . past the Bank of Indiana and
the Masonic Temple and the YMCA. Five blocks later
I ran into the lobby of the Sheraton.

When I got to my room I dialed Information.

A voice with a Midwestern accent asked, "What
city, please?"

"Auburn," I said. "The telephone number for Edith
Carnahan."

I listened while the operator leafed through the
pages of her directory. Finally she said, "I'm sorry,
sir. I have no listing for an Edith Carnahan."

Forty-seven years, I thought. How many persons
stay in one place that long?

"Are there *any* Carnahans in Auburn?"

"Let's see. Yessir, there are six."

"Operator," I said anxiously, "give me all six numbers, please."

"I'm sorry," she said, "company rules permit us to give only three numbers at a time."

"Operator," I said, my voice rising, "this is an emergency—"

"I'll have to check with my supervisor."

"Hurry . . . please." I waited.

"My supervisor wants to know what kind of emergency this is."

"I'm trying to save a life!" I said.

She repeated my message to her supervisor. Then she said, "Yes, sir, we will make that exception."

She recited the numbers. I jotted them down. And then I began telephoning. A woman answered the first call. I asked if she knew an Edith Carnahan.

"She used to live in Auburn," I said.

"Don't believe I do. Edith? No, I'm afraid I never knew anybody by that name."

I dialed the next number. A man said, "Who'd y' say you was lookin' for?"

"Edith Carnahan."

"Never heard o' her."

"It's been a long time," I said.

"How long?"

"Almost fifty years."

"Fifty years! Good grief, man, she could be dead!"

I called two other numbers. No luck. On my fifth call, a woman said she thought the name sounded familiar.

"I'm not a Carnahan myself," she said, "but I'm

married to one. Seems to me, though, I've heard my husband speak of kin named Edith."

He was in the fields, she explained. "But if you can call back at noon you can speak to him."

"At noon?"

"Yes, he'll be home for dinner then. Maybe he can help you."

I called again at precisely twelve o'clock. This time the woman's husband answered.

"Why, sure," he said. "Used to be an Edith Carnahan lived here in Auburn. Can't say whether she still does, though. My gosh, it's been years since I've heard that name."

"Was Carnahan her married name?"

"No," he said, "seems to me . . . let me think. Oh, sure, I remember now. She was married to a feller name of Newcomb." He spelled it for me: "N-E-W-C-O-M-B."

"Thanks," I said. "I'm terribly grateful."

Hurriedly I dialed Information again. "Operator, would you please give me the telephone number for Edith Newcomb in Auburn."

I heard her leafing through her directory. Finally she said, "I show no listing for an Edith Newcomb in Auburn."

"Are you certain, operator?"

"Positive, sir. Could it be a new listing?"

"I doubt it. But please check it anyway."

I heard the pages turning again and then she came back on the line. "No, there's nothing."

"Operator, maybe it's spelled differently. . . ?"

Finally she said, "Well, sir, I have an Edith Neukom. It's spelled N-E-U-K-O-M."

"In Auburn?"

"Yes, sir, in Auburn."

Edith *Neukom,* not *Newcomb.*

That explained it! This *had* to be the woman I was searching for. This must be Jody's mother!

My hand was shaking so I could hardly write. I jotted down the address and telephone number. I wouldn't call, I decided. There was no telling how she would react. I didn't want to frighten her. It wouldn't make sense to call a perfect stranger and say, "Hello, Mother. This is your son-in-law speaking!"

Downstairs I looked around for a taxi.

"There's a convention," the doorman said. "Looks like they're all busy."

I took off down Washington Boulevard on the run and kept right on running until I was seven blocks away, standing before a sign that read HERTZ RENT-A-CAR.

6:30 A.M.

When Aunt Betty told him he had a sister, Carny promised himself he'd find her some day. Aunt Betty said she was a twin. So he watched wherever he went, looking for somebody who was a look-alike. He used to wonder if she might be living in Auburn. That was what troubled him most when his grandparents took him away to Elwood. He figured maybe he was leaving his sister behind.

Once, when he was older, he searched for his sister

in Erie, Pennsylvania. For some reason, his Aunt Betty had the idea that was where the people took her, the ones who adopted her. Another time, Aunt Betty said she'd heard his sister was an airline stewardess living in New York. So after the war Carny went there too. But of course it was useless, because he didn't even know her name. Anyway, he kept on walking the streets, looking for a woman who looked like him.

Now, after all the years, Carny had gotten over the idea of ever finding her. He ran a hand through his hair. He noticed that it was starting to thin. He rubbed his eyes. He was getting too old for dreams any more, he told himself; too old to believe any of them ever came true.

Carny looked up at the kitchen clock. He'd been sitting there for more than three hours. Now he could hear Beulah stirring in the other room.

She poked her head through the door. "My goodness, Bob Carnahan, you never comin' back to bed?"

He shook his head. "I've just been settin' here thinkin'. You go on back, Beulah—I just want to think some more."

He stood now, shuffled over to the stove, and poured himself another cup of coffee.

12

LEAVING FORT WAYNE, I swung north onto Highway 27. Auburn lay straight ahead. The road cut through rural countryside typical of Indiana—dairy cows grazing in the fields and Amish buggies rolling along the edges of the road. Dogs chased after the carriages and crows scolded from the trees, and framing the entire scene were pasturelands spreading clear to the horizon: soft green carpets under a cornflower sky. I thought of the chaotic freeways of Los Angeles —cars roaring, time racing. And somewhere in the same city, I knew an operating room was waiting for Jody. As the minutes raced by, she moved closer, closer to that room.

I had been driving for nearly an hour when a sign loomed ahead on the right side of the road: "Welcome to Auburn, the Classic Car Capital of the World." It was here, a generation ago, that the Auburn automobile was assembled . . . along with the Cord and the

Duesenberg. Now the old cars are displayed in a museum on the approach to town.

I drove along streets lined with elms. Rows of white frame houses stood stiffly behind them, old-fashioned swings almost frivolous in their presence on the porches.

I was looking for a woman named Edith Neukom and all I had was a route number. I parked the car across the street from the courthouse and went into a drugstore.

The saleslady shook her head. "Edith Neukom? No. Don't believe I ever heard of her."

"She's lived here a long time," I explained.

"Long? How long?"

"Well, fifty years probably."

"Oh, my. Someone should know her."

I started to say I have a route number, but she interrupted. "Why don't you try the post office? That's your best bet."

But it turned out to be a city holiday, and the post office was closed. I walked up the street to a grocery and handed the clerk a slip of paper with Mrs. Neukom's name on it.

He studied it for a minute. "Sounds familiar." He scratched his head. "Just can't place her, though."

I was beginning to panic. What if I couldn't find Edith Neukom? Maybe the telephone operator had been wrong.

I drove to a service station. "I'm looking for a woman named Edith Neukom," I told the attendant. "She lives on Route Four. . . ."

"She a little woman?" he asked.

I told him I didn't know.

"Well, if she's the one I think she is, she lives right at the top of that next hill." He pointed. "A little white bungalow up there. Sits all alone."

I found the house—a simple frame cottage surrounded by pines and maples. Her name was on the mailbox. A big sycamore hung over the roof like an umbrella, and squirrels scampered through the yard, chasing one another through the thick grass. I turned off the ignition and sat quietly for a moment. It was hot. Muggy and hot. The back of my shirt was wet with perspiration. I could feel my heart racing wildly and my throat was dry, terribly dry. How do you walk up to someone's door and tear away the cobwebs of a lifetime? As a reporter, I'd had the unpleasant task of delivering shocking news to families—about an accident, or a shooting, or a kidnapping. But now I was *involved*—it was Jody's story; hers and mine.

I got out of the car and started toward the house, and as I walked up the path toward the porch, all the courage suddenly left me. I wanted to run but I couldn't. What was I going to say to the woman inside this little cottage, about a daughter she'd never known? Was I to say that Jody was a mother now herself, and that at this very moment she lay near death . . . but that before she died she demanded some answers: she wanted to know why she was given away and who her mother was and what she looked like (was she short, tall, gray, blonde?) and whether she had dimples and the same sad dark eyes that would fill with tears when she let herself wonder . . . And did she have the same small feet, and was she also sensitive, and were there other children, and, God, dear God, please, had she ever regretted giving her baby away?

I stood on the porch. The door was open. Peering through the screen, I saw a woman. She was seated on a couch, sewing, and next to her was a young boy. She came to the door—a small woman, smaller than Jody; and her eyes were blue, not brown like Jody's; and her hair was auburn, not dark like Jody's.

I glanced nervously at the boy on the davenport. I had wanted to question her alone.

"Mrs. Neukom?"

I had a plan which I'd rehearsed in the event she wasn't alone.

"Yes."

"I'm looking for Edith Carnahan. She used to go to school with my mother."

The woman smiled. "Why, that was my maiden name. What was your mother's?"

"Elena. Elena Bates."

The woman thought for a moment. "Mmm, I don't seem to recall anybody by that name."

It all seemed so unreal. It was as if this little porch were a stage, and I was in the audience, waiting for something thunderously dramatic to happen. Again I had the urge to get away, but now the woman was speaking.

"Now you come on inside and cool off," she said. "It's too darn hot to be standin' out there on that porch." She introduced me to the boy. "That there's my grandson," she said proudly.

She motioned me to a sofa and then went to a

closet and got out several old photo albums. Then, seated next to me, she began turning the pages.

"Now you just tell me when you see your mother's picture," she said. I watched, fascinated, as she turned the pages, pointing to photos of herself as a young girl. The resemblance to Jody was startling, even though her coloring wasn't the same. Soon it became a game. She'd hold up a class picture and ask, "Can you figure out which one is me?"

It was simple, for throughout the album she had the same sad-happy smile in each picture, even as a youngster, which told you that life hadn't been pleasant for this woman.

She offered me a cup of coffee, but I said no. I would return later, I decided, when she was alone, after her grandson had gone. I pretended there was a picture album I wanted to pick up at my hotel. "I'll see you in an hour or so," I told her as the screen door closed behind me.

In Auburn I walked around the old courthouse. It sits on a grassy square surrounded on four sides by streets and shops. On the lawn there's a memorial to the local servicemen who died in recent wars. Auburn is one of those Midwestern towns where everyone is genuinely proud to be an American, and they still honor their dead. Those who gave their lives for their country aren't forgotten. In a town like this nothing is ever forgotten, really. I could sense it all around me. The past. My wife's past, too. It was here. I knew that now.

I kept walking until I found a telephone. I wanted to tell someone I had found her, found Jody's mother.

I decided to call Dr. Marxer, but all I got was the answering service. I left word to say I had called and that I would telephone the doctor at home in the evening.

Rounding a corner, I went into a restaurant and ordered a sandwich and coffee. My hand shook as I picked up the cup. I looked at my watch. It had been less than an hour since I'd left Mrs. Neukom's. I wanted to wait until I was sure she was alone. I finished my sandwich and then took a stroll around Auburn. I still had time to kill, so I ducked into a tavern on Cedar Street and took a stool near the door. A couple of guys were playing a pinball machine, and a radio was blaring country music.

"Hi," the countergirl said pleasantly. "What'll it be?"

"A beer," I said.

"Bottled or draft?"

"Draft."

She slid the beer across the counter. "You're not from around here—tell the truth."

"California," I said. "Just arrived a couple of days ago."

"Hey now, what you up to around here, California?"

She was a simple, pleasant girl in her way, refreshing to talk to.

"I'm chasing a name—somebody's past."

She stepped back, hands on her hips. "Wow," she said, "now who you chasin', sport?"

I sipped my beer. "A ghost," I said.

She gave me a hard look then. "Hey, don't fun with me, mister."

I gave her a hard look back. "Little lady," I said, "the fact is I'm not funning with you one bit."

She looked at me and shrugged. "What part of California you from?"

"Los Angeles."

"Hey, that's near Hollywood, right?"

"Correct."

"Know any movie stars?"

I shrugged. "A few."

"Hey, I'm going there some day."

"Oh?"

"Damn right. I sing a little, dance a little," she smiled. "Maybe I can get into pictures."

I finished my beer and looked at my watch. It was three o'clock. I'd been gone from Mrs. Neukom's for nearly two hours. I paid for the beer and drove slowly back to the white cottage. Mrs. Neukom was standing on the porch.

"I thought you maybe decided not to come back," she said as she held the door for me and led me inside. "I'll warm some coffee."

The house was extraordinarily clean. On the living room TV stood pictures of her sons, and other family photos hung on the walls.

Mrs. Neukom came back with a tray. "Do you take cream and sugar in your coffee?"

I shook my head. "No, just black, thanks."

She sat beside me on the davenport. "Now, let's see those pictures you brought."

"Mrs. Neukom," I began slowly, "I'm here for another reason, and it has nothing to do with pictures."

She looked at me with sudden alarm. "I'm afraid I don't understand—"

I handed her the copy of Jody's amended birth certificate. She looked at it curiously.

"Mrs. Neukom," I said gently, "does that mean anything to you?"

She shook her head. "No . . ."

"Doesn't the date . . . ?"

"No, I don't know what you mean."

She handed the certificate back to me and I gave her Dr. Marxer's letter. Her hand was trembling. I had no doubts now. This was Jody's real mother. But I wanted her to tell me. I wanted to be able to go home, to say, "Jody, I found your mother and, yes, she's a dear lady, and, no, she didn't want to give you away"; to say, "Jody, it was all just a set of tragic circumstances and no one is to blame, Jody, no one."

But Mrs. Neukom remained silent.

Finally I told her that my wife was adopted, that her real mother was from Auburn and that her name was Edith Carnahan.

Mrs. Neukom faced me. "Why, that couldn't be," she said.

I stood up. "Mrs. Neukom, I've been to the courthouse in Fort Wayne. I've checked the records."

The woman shook her head again. "It must be someone else. Someone with the same name."

"Mrs. Neukom," I said very gently again, "my wife is ill, critically ill. She's dying, right this minute, and it's important that the doctors know more about her family—her *real* family. I need your help and my wife needs your help. The doctors must have your medical records. . . ."

She stared at the floor for a long time. When at last she spoke, it was the voice of someone coming out of a long trance, someone released from a dream forty-

seven years old. Yes, she *was* Edith Carnahan. Yes, she
had given her daughter up for adoption. The story
spilled out of her now without pause—a confession,
an appeal for forgiveness, for understanding.

"I didn't want to give her away," the woman sobbed.
"That's the God's honest truth. We were poor and my
parents made me do it. I never even got to see her.
The people who adopted her took that baby away
from me so fast." She looked up. "I want you to know
this—I wanted to keep her, I swear before God. I've
never stopped praying for that child. I've cried my
heart out. . . ."

Suddenly the room fell silent. The whole meaning
of my search suddenly seemed distilled in that brief
moment.

But Mrs. Neukom wasn't finished; there was something else. Jody had a brother, she said, a twin. His
name was Robert, Robert Carnahan, and her parents
had reared him.

"They gave my little girl away," she said, "and they
kept Robert and they taught him that I didn't love
him. . . . I married a man named Reno Neukom. We
had two sons, but I hardly ever got to see Robert. Oh,
that boy had an awful childhood, and then he went
away to war and was wounded, and then he came
back around here for a little while, left again, and I
just don't know where he is."

She looked at me, the tragedy reflected in her eyes.
"He's been gone seventeen years, that boy, and I just
don't know where to look or anything."

I asked her if Jody's father was still alive. No, he
was dead, died of a stroke three years ago. Her eyes

said she didn't want to talk about it, that she was happy he was gone, happy and relieved.

I looked at my watch. It was five o'clock. I asked Mrs. Neukom about her medical history. She'd had a stroke a year ago, she said, and, yes, she'd had dizzy spells all her life and lately a strange numbness . . . just as Jody had. Carefully I wrote down her prescriptions and the name of her doctor. Then I put my notebook away. It was time to go. Before leaving, I asked her for a picture. "It would please Jody," I said. She searched, but she couldn't find anything recent. So I drove into Auburn, to the same drugstore where I'd inquired about her earlier, and I bought an Instamatic and a roll of film, and on the way back I stopped at a florist and bought her a terrarium, and later, after taking her picture, I leaned down and kissed her on the forehead. She looked up, her eyes flooding with tears again, and then she pressed something into my hand.

"For my baby," she said. "I crocheted it and I want her to have it, please."

She squeezed my hand.

It was only later, when I was outside, back in the car, that I looked to see what she had slipped into my hand.

It was a dishcloth—a simple dishcloth.

"For my baby," she had said.

13

DRIVING BACK TO FORT WAYNE, I
watched the sun disappear into a distant cornfield.
Jody had her identity, but would she live to make it
matter—after all the years of wondering?

Back at the hotel, I telephoned the hospital. The
nurse told me Jody wasn't taking any calls, that she'd
had an angiogram and the doctor had ordered absolute
quiet. "She's very weak," the nurse said, "and the dizzy
spells have worsened."

"Is she sleeping?" I asked.

"No, she's resting."

"Let me speak to her, nurse, please. I'm her husband. . . it's very important."

"All right, Mr. Hulse—but please don't be long."

There was a pause, and then I heard Jody say
weakly, "Hi, where are you?"

"Still in Indiana, honey."

"You sound excited."

"Jo, I found her—"

"My mother?"

"Your mother, I found her!"

"Oh, Jerry!"

"I found her!"

"What's she like?"

I described the tiny woman, and the house, and the yard with the squirrels and the big sycamore out front.

"Did she want to know . . . about me?"

"She said she didn't want to give you away."

"But, why. . . ?"

"Her parents made her do it."

She was sobbing. "Oh, Jerry, my mother . . ."

"Little Jo," I finally said, "I'm coming home now. You rest, honey—I'll see you tomorrow."

I called Dr. Marxer and told him about Mrs. Neukom's illnesses. I read him the prescriptions from my notebook as he took notes.

"Has she ever had a stroke?" he asked.

"Yes, about a year ago."

"Serious?"

"Apparently not."

"What about the father?" he asked.

"Dead."

"How long ago?"

"About three years."

"Of what?"

"A stroke."

"How old was he?"

I said that Jody's mother seemed to think he was about eighty-two. "She wasn't sure. Maybe eighty-three."

He explained that this was excellent news; that although both parents had suffered strokes, and even though the father had died of one, there was longevity in each parent, no history of *early* death from vascular disease. Jody stood a chance. If she could make it through the operation, she could, with proper medication, perhaps live a relatively normal life span. But he reminded me that Jody was critically ill and so he made no promises—anything could happen.

"I'm glad to have the medical history . . . we can use it," he said. "But what's really important is that you've given her a will to survive, to live, and right now that's very necessary."

Later I went back to the bar on the roof of the Sheraton.

The bartender waved. "Still with us?"

"One more night."

"What'll it be?"

"Scotch. Make it a double."

Pouring the drink, he said, "So you're going home tomorrow."

"Yes, but I'll be coming back."

I turned and studied the city. It was all familiar now, this place that had seemed a strange force working against me only a day or two ago. I recognized the streets and buildings, and I thought about all of the lives that had touched Jody's: "Mother Mac," who'd first held her; the attorney who "legalized" the tragic mother-daughter separation; the doctor who'd delivered her and later committed suicide; and Judge Celarek, that good and human man.

"Another Scotch?" the bartender asked.

"No, thanks," I said. "I've had it for tonight."

Back in my room, I looked out at the city again. The rain had stopped and the skies were clearing. A full moon shone on the courthouse. Funny, I thought, how friendly that old building seemed now. Then, as I was turning out the light, I saw it—the package from Jody's mother, the dishcloth. It still lay carefully folded on the bedside table, a simple token of love that took more than two-score years to bestow.

For the first time in many years, Edith Neukom was at peace. Lying in bed, she said her prayers. And just as she had done each night since Jody was born, she asked God to watch over her "little girl." Only tonight she gave thanks that He had found Jody for her. And it was then that all the memories came flooding back. Jody's father had been a neighbor, a married man who owned a farm nearby, and one day her mother sent Edith to buy butter and the man flirted, reached and made to grab Edith, so she took the butter and ran. She was only fifteen years old; but after that, whenever she passed anywhere near that man, he'd call to her and she'd run like the devil. He was a handsome man, that one, and smart with the words, but she hated him, and was afraid—and one time she was coming home from school and he chased her, and she ran out through the cow pasture, him laughing and calling for her to come back. Every time she walked by he'd call out, "Hey, Edith," and try to coax her into the barn.

When her folks asked her to go after butter again, she said no. Finally, though, one day she was passing his farm and he came out with a pitchfork, and when she saw him with the pitchfork she froze. "C'mere," he said, only this time he wasn't smilin'. She started to run but he shouted, "Stop or I'll kill ya!" and she dropped her books and then she just fell down where she stood and when she looked up he was standing over her saying, "Git up!" and when she didn't move he reached down and pulled her to her feet and marched her into the barn, and when she tried to shout he put his hand over her mouth and then he tore her clothes off. Afterward he told her he'd kill her if she ever told.

When she found out she was expecting and she told her ma, her ma said, "You coulda run!" But nobody did anything because everybody was afraid of that man. So she just went to that home, that maternity home in Fort Wayne, and she had those babies, those twin babies, only the strangers took the girl baby away and her parents took the boy, Robert, and made her go to work to support him, and later he went his way, too.

Even after her husband died and she still wanted Robert, her parents said no. She never did get over the death of Reno Neukom. She loved that man. Forty years since he'd passed away and she'd never re-married. Together they'd built this house where she still lived, and even though they'd been poor, they were happy. Then one day he stepped on a nail and he got terribly ill. Lockjaw's what the doctor called it. He was thirty-one. They took him to the hospital and she stayed up with him night and day until finally, the doctor said, "Edith, go home and get some rest. There's nothing you can do here." And so she'd gone home. Only later she wished she'd stayed because it was only a little while till a neighbor woman came over. The doctor had phoned her and the woman had tears in her eyes. She told her, "Edith, he's gone. Reno's dead."

She wanted to die, right then, she wanted to die that very moment, but she kept on living. The funeral was on a Saturday and she went to work the following Monday because all she had left after paying for the funeral was forty dollars.

14

BOB CARNAHAN COULDN'T SLEEP. The locusts in the tree outside his trailer were like a million crickets singing all at once. But it wasn't just that. He was thinking about his mother. For the first time in months, he was wondering if she was well and what she was doing. It had been seventeen years since he'd seen her. He remembered how he'd always wanted to live with her when he was a little boy. But each time he would tell his grandmother this, the old woman would shake her head and say, "Robert, I just don't understand you. Why do you want to go there? Your mother doesn't want you, she doesn't want to be bothered with you. How many times do you have to be told that?"

Bob Carnahan couldn't recall ever hearing the word "love" spoken in his grandparents' home. Not one single time. When he wasn't going to school he was in the fields, shocking wheat or planting tomatoes. In the summertime he was in the fields all day long. He'd done this since he was seven years old.

Everything he earned, his grandparents took. Even once when he wanted a nickel for Sunday School they refused. The money he earned, they said, was for his board.

One summer, though, his grandmother promised him that if he worked extra hard she'd buy him a bicycle. It was then that he began plotting how he'd run off with his new bike and visit his mother. He spent weeks planning the trip. At night when his grandparents thought he was asleep he'd get out the map he'd hidden under the mattress and he'd study the route to Auburn. He figured it was about a hundred miles to his mother's house.

That summer he worked every single day. Even Sundays. Sometimes at night he'd be so exhausted he'd go to bed without taking his clothes off. Other times, tired as he was, he'd lie awake thinking about the bike and the trip to Auburn. He worked ten hours a day, all summer long. By September he'd earned more than two hundred and fifty dollars, and his grandmother bought him the bicycle, just as she'd promised she would. She paid twenty-four dollars for it. The rest she kept for board.

He remembered the morning he ran away. It was still dark outside, not yet four o'clock. He slipped out the back door and the screen made a squeaking noise and he was scared to death he'd awakened his grandparents. For a couple of minutes he didn't even breathe. Then, when he was sure no one had heard him, he jumped on the bicycle and pedaled away.

All he brought with him was what he wore—a pair of jeans, a denim work shirt, and a pair of sneakers with a hole in one toe. This and a few crackers, and an apple. He wanted to get as far away as possible before his grandparents woke up and saw he was gone. They'd call the police. He was sure of that.

He looked around. The moon was shining and the fields were all coated with silver. Later, though, it got hot. It was one of those sweltering Indiana mornings. All day long he pedaled. He rode through Marion and Rockcreek and Huntington and Garrett. The only time he stopped was to eat. The rest of the day he rode, right up till dark. It was late when he finally got to Auburn. He put his bike behind his mother's house and knocked on the door. When she answered, well, she just stood there for a minute with her mouth open, and then all of a sudden she grabbed him and was kissing him and hugging him and kissing him.

He told her how he'd run away because he just had to see her, and afterward she told him that she'd gone to a fortuneteller and the fortuneteller had told her she was going to see a son who'd been gone for a long, long time. But she was surprised even so.

She warmed over some stew and then they talked till after midnight. When he finally went to bed, Robert Carnahan was the happiest he'd ever been.

This lasted for only a couple of days because then his grandparents came and took him back. Even though his mother argued, they made him go. They took his bike away too. They locked it up in the barn.

A couple of years later he ran away a second time. This time he hitchhiked to Auburn. It was midmorning when he left the farm and he caught a ride with a truck driver all the way to Fort Wayne. From there he got another lift into Auburn. It was raining, one of those heavy rains that come to Indiana in the summertime. Going through the town he was careful no one saw him. He was afraid that if somebody did they might call the police and he'd have to go back to Elwood. For more than an hour he hid out in a field. Then about two o'clock he cut through a farmer's place and ran straight to his mother's house. He was soaked when he got there. He knocked on the door but no one answered.

It was unlocked, so he let himself inside. Everything was dead quiet. He called out, but no one was home. His mother was working, he figured, and his half brothers were in school. He crossed the room and flopped down on the davenport. The quiet made him uneasy. He'd never felt so lonely, even though he'd been lonely all his life. In his head he used to make up pictures of the sister his Aunt Betty had told him about. He didn't know the name of his twin, so he made that up too. He called his sister Mary. Sometimes he pretended he and Mary were playing together and they'd have the best times. And then it would come to him that it was all made up.

Now, seated on the davenport in his mother's home, he began thinking about all those lonely years, and suddenly the hurt he'd felt got all knotted up and his shoulders began shaking and a scream rose in him and it came out of his mouth and was followed by another and he was screaming to God that he wanted to die. And all of a sudden he knew what he'd never admitted before—that nobody really wanted him, nobody in the world. The rain poured down outside, and he just got up and went to the bathroom and opened the cabinet over the sink. And then he just reached inside and got a razor and he just raised it up and stuck it deep inside his throat.

He'd expected it to hurt, but it only stung. But it was bleeding bad and he was getting dizzy. He staggered out of the bathroom and into the living room and then onto the back porch and from there he struggled up the ladder and into the attic. That's where he wanted to die. He crawled to a corner behind some boxes and he just huddled in there so death could come and get him.

But it was his mother who came to get him. The door opened downstairs and he heard his mother screaming and he figured she'd seen the blood leading to the attic.

Later, when he was all healed and had gotten back his strength, he went away to the Army. He just left it all behind him—or anyway, he tried to—and just went away the best he could.

15

THE TELEPHONE RANG beside my bed. It was the hotel operator. "Good morning, sir, this is your wake-up call." I looked at my watch. Seven thirty. My mind was fuzzy. I hadn't fallen asleep until nearly dawn. I raised the blinds. It was misty outside. I prayed my flight wouldn't be delayed. This was Thursday. Twenty-four hours and Jody would be in surgery.

I showered and shaved and hurried downstairs to the lobby. The bellhop carried my bags to the door, motioning to a taxi.

"Where to?" the driver asked.

"The courthouse, then the airport," I said.

The skies were slowly clearing and the sun was beginning to shine.

"Looks like it'll be a nice day after all," the driver said.

"Hope so," I said, my mind on Jody and the operation tomorrow.

He dropped me at the courthouse on Calhoun Street.

"I'll only be a minute," I called back as I hurried up the marble steps. By now sunlight was streaming through the stained glass window in the courthouse dome, flooding the rotunda with that cathedral light. I opened Judge Celarek's door. He was seated behind his desk, going through his morning mail.

"Good morning, Frank."

He looked up and smiled. "Why, hello, Jerry."

"Busy?" I said.

He gestured with the letter opener. "Not too busy to talk to you. Sit down."

"I've only got a few minutes," I said. "There's a taxi waiting."

"You're going home today?"

"I'm on my way to the airport now."

"So the search was successful?"

"With your help, yes."

"Talk to Jody?"

"Yes, last night."

"And?"

"She said to tell you . . . thanks."

He smiled broadly. "You tell her that's okay, hear?"

"I will, Frank. . . . I must go. I just wanted to . . ."

He walked with me to the door. "I know." He put out his hand.

"I'll write," I said.

"Good. Keep me posted."

As the cab pulled away I looked back at the courthouse and read the inscription below the dome: "Justice—the hope for all who suffer." Corny? I didn't think so, no, and I still don't think so.

Six hours later my plane began its descent into Los Angeles International Airport. I gazed out the window. Far to the north, through the smog, I could make out the sprawling complex of St. John's Hospital.

At the terminal I claimed my luggage and then hailed a cab. It was only three o'clock, but already the traffic was a nightmare. It was stop and go for an hour, all the way to the hospital.

I stopped at the nurse's station on the way to Jody's room. I could see the concern in the nurse's eyes. The dizziness had worsened, she said. Jody had fainted earlier in the afternoon while undergoing laboratory tests for tomorrow's surgery.

I went quickly along the corridor to her room. She was white. So white that her face was almost indistinct against the pillow. By now she was unable even to sit up. I leaned down and kissed her. Her face was damp and she was weak, frightfully weak.

"I'm so glad you're back," Jody said, her voice scarcely audible.

I took her hand. "It's going to be okay, Little Jo, everything's going to be okay after tomorrow."

"I hope so," Jody said. But I knew she didn't really think so.

I reached in my pocket and pulled out the dishcloth. Removing the tissue, I placed the gift in her hands.

"From my mother?"

I nodded. "She sends it to her daughter . . . with all her love."

"Did she make it?"

"She crocheted it for you."

She hugged it to her, a simple dishcloth. I believe

that at that very moment Jody was happier than she'd ever been in her entire life.

"Tell me again," she said. "Tell me about my mother."

Jody spoke the word "mother" with the reverence one reserves for speaking of God.

I recited everything I had said on the telephone the night before. I described the house again and the yard again and the trees where the squirrels play.

"Your mother feeds the squirrels every morning and again in the afternoon," I said. "They hop right up on the porch. There's one she calls Red. He's something special, I guess."

Jody smiled and hugged the dishcloth again, proof to her that in this world a woman lived who was her real mother.

Moments later the attending surgeon asked if I would step outside. Earlier in the week Jody had undergone an angiogram, a complicated X ray in which dye is injected into the bloodstream in order to locate the problem area. The doctor told me that the blockage was found at the base of Jody's brain. The artery was nearly shut off. Only a hairline flow of blood was seeping through, which accounted for the dizziness, the fainting spells, the blurred vision, the slurred speech. Jody's brain was starving for oxygen. If the artery closed off completely, she'd suffer a stroke. This would mean death or crippling, a fear that had haunted her these last weeks.

After the surgeon had gone, Jody had a second visitor, a woman she'd known a long time ago, but right away she began talking about courage and facing death, and I thought, "Oh, forget it!" and suddenly I wished to hell our old pastor, Ray Wallace, was there, because he'd know the right things to say and it wouldn't involve any litany on death.

When "Mrs. Smiles" left, I figured Jody needed some cheering up.

"Remember our honeymoon?" I asked.

"Yes."

"Betcha can't remember what we had for our wedding breakfast."

"Jelly rolls and Pepsi-Cola!"

"Right."

She laughed. "What was that car you were driving when we were married?"

"That wasn't a car, lady, it was a limousine! A 'thirty-five Ford. Ripple discs on the wheels. Skirts on the fenders. I could have had any girl in town with that wagon!"

"Quit bragging."

Then I said, "I didn't want any other girl, Jo . . . I only wanted you."

She paused. "Jerry?"

I knew what was coming. "Yes?"

"If anything happens, Jerry, well, I don't want you to, well, to grieve."

"Maybe you'd prefer that I celebrate?" I said, forcing the joke while the lump in my throat grew bigger.

"Look, I don't want to be a cripple," she said.

"You're not going to be a cripple, Jo, you're going to live and be healthy . . . the doctor said so. . . ."

She squeezed my hand. "Jerry, take good care of yourself, promise?"

I could feel the tightening in my throat again, so I turned and stared out the window.

"Jerry?"

"Uh-huh."

"Don't look so sad."

I smiled. "I'm not sad, just tired. You know, the trip and all."

"Get some rest, Jerry."

When my wife said that, I went out to the car and cried. I cried for us all—for Jody, myself, our sons, and for a tiny woman who feeds squirrels and crochets dishcloths and who lives in a doll house in Auburn, Indiana.

16

THE SURGERY WAS SCHEDULED for eight A.M. With our youngest son, Bo, I was at the hospital by seven o'clock. Our other son, Dick, was teaching school in Australia and Jody had made me promise not to tell him of her illness, and I had kept my promise.

She was already heavily sedated when Bo and I arrived at her bedside. Two nurses were with her. One was measuring Jody's blood pressure, the other marking a chart. Jody's eyes were glazed, her lids fluttering open and shut, and she was fighting to remain awake.

At exactly seven thirty, two male attendants in surgical caps and gowns wheeled a stretcher into the room. It was time for her to go. They lowered the railing around her bed. They lifted Jody onto the stretcher. Bo and I leaned over and kissed her one last time. Her lips were moving. She was trying to say goodbye.

I stroked her hair and in my mind I saw her walking

toward high school on that gray morning so many years before. I heard the wind blowing and Jody saying, "No, thank you," when I offered her the ride. And in my memory I watched her draw her sweater up tightly around her neck while the wind gusted, mussing her hair, and I drove away.

Now the silky dark hair was streaked with gray and her lips were pale, and this was another goodbye, perhaps the last. Bo and I followed the stretcher down the hall. We watched while the elevator doors opened and then closed, and Jody was gone. Just as the doors shut, I noticed something, something she held in her hand.

It was the dishcloth.

The operation would be a long one, the surgeon had said. In the visitors' room I looked at my watch. It was eight o'clock. By now Jody would be in a deep sleep. I offered up a silent prayer—and then I left Bo and walked slowly along the corridor to the hospital entrance. Standing in the doorway, I watched the traffic hurrying along Santa Monica Boulevard, and I was reminded how lost one human can be in a big city. As a young reporter, I once covered a suicide on this same busy boulevard—a destitute old woman who'd gotten herself all gussied up in her finest nightgown and then swallowed a couple of dozen sleeping pills. While she was waiting for them to send her off to whatever awaited her in the next world, she wrote out a "confession." The note found at her bedside told how she'd "committed the crime of growing old." She was lonely, she said, terribly, terribly lonely. Imagine. Somebody living on this bustling boulevard, with hundreds of other human beings passing her door every hour, yet she was lonely. That's right. There was just one minor problem: nobody ever knocked.

Now, waiting for the operation to be over, I realized how much love really means and how alone you can be without it. Some of us are lucky; a few care. But if you're like the poor old lady who took all those pills, life can be empty. Even on a crowded street.

I walked back to the waiting room. There were others there—some reading, some sleeping. All of them worrying. I tried to concentrate on a magazine, but it was useless. Bo sat beside me on the leather lounge. We were silent. We could not speak.

In an attempt to take my mind off the operation, I recalled the time Jody and I became "celebrities" during the grand opening of the Beverly Hilton Hotel. It was a black-tie affair, and my city editor had asked me to go in his place.

"But Mr. Lewis," I protested, "I don't own a tux."

He shrugged. "Wear a dark suit and a bow tie. Nobody'll notice."

He handed me a police sticker. "For your windshield," he said. "It'll get you by the cops."

So the next evening Jody and I piled into our vintage Chevrolet with its banged-up front fenders and busted headlight and headed off to Beverly Hills. As we turned onto Wilshire Boulevard, the car started hissing and missing.

Jody looked at me. "Is it going to stall?"

I was too tense to answer. We turned into the Beverly Hilton drive, and joined a line of Rolls Royces and Bentleys and Cadillacs. A cop looked at me suspiciously, but when he saw the sticker he waved me on. My plan was to park the car deep in the lot, where nobody would notice.

"We'll have to walk," I told Jody.

She shook her head. "I don't mind."

As it turned out, we didn't have to walk anywhere, because just as I was pulling out of line, another cop blew his whistle and waved me back in.

I leaned out the window. "I want to park it myself," I shouted.

He shouted back, "You can't. Anyone with one of those stickers has got to stay in line. They'll park it for you, buddy." He pointed toward the hotel.

I looked ahead. "Oh, no!"

"Oh, no," Jody echoed.

Bleachers had been installed in front of the hotel. They were jammed with movie fans, and each time a film star alighted from a limousine the people in the bleachers would holler their heads off. Not only that, there were three coachmen who blasted away on trumpets with the arrival of each car.

"I can't believe it," Jody said. "Get us out of here!"

"Can't," I said. "We're stuck."

We were wedged between two Cadillac limousines. The car ahead of us stopped. The trumpets sounded. The occupants stepped out. The fans cheered.

"Oh, God, please," I muttered to myself.

It was our turn next, and I'm still not certain who made the greater racket—the trumpeters, or the fans who roared when a parking attendant attempted to dislodge Jody. In our panic, we'd forgotten—her handle was missing and the door was roped shut.

The attendant pulled gently at first. Then he jerked harder. Another attendant ran around the car to assist him. I tried to explain. They wouldn't listen. They pulled, they tugged, they cursed.

"Oh, forget it," I said finally.

I hit the accelerator. The car lurched forward. Tires screeching, I roared out the driveway, leaving behind the fans, the trumpeters, and the parking attendants, in a huge cloud of dirty black smoke.

Out on Wilshire Boulevard again, I turned to Jody. We began to laugh. We absolutely broke up. We were still laughing as the comic Chevy, steaming and hissing, delivered us faithfully home. . . .

I glanced at the clock in the hospital waiting room. Nine fifteen. I went to the reception desk.

A nurse looked up. "Yes?"

"My wife, is there any news yet?"

She shook her head. "We'll call you just as soon as Mrs. Hulse is out of surgery."

Back in the waiting room, Bo put a hand on my shoulder. "Can I get you some coffee?" he asked.

"Thanks," I said, "not now."

I glanced down at my watch again. The second hand seemed to be standing still. I leaned back and closed my eyes. Then Bo was touching my arm. Looking up, I saw the same nurse I'd spoken to earlier.

"Mr. Hulse . . ."

I jumped to my feet. "Yes?"

"Would you step this way, please? Your doctor would like to see you."

He stood just outside the door, still in his surgical gown.

We shook hands. "My wife—how is she?" I asked anxiously.

"She came through pretty well," the doctor said, removing his surgical cap.

"Will she . . . live?"

He nodded. "I believe so."

"When can we see her?" I asked.

"She'll be going to intensive care soon," he said. "If you wait here, they'll be wheeling her by any minute."

We saw her coming. Her throat was heavily bandaged, and she was moaning. One of the attendants held a plasma bottle over Jody's head.

In the intensive care unit, four electrodes were attached to Jody's body, carrying her heartbeat to a cardioscope behind her bed. If her heart should stop, an alarm would signal doctors, nurses, inhalation therapists, and other members of a life-saving team. I stood watching the cardioscope. Jody's heartbeat passed across its screen like the blip on a radarscope.

I stood beside Jody's bed and pressed her hand.

"Don't let go," she whispered. "I'm afraid. . . ."

"I won't ever let go," I said softly. "You're going to live. Besides, there's someone waiting for you . . . the Squirrel Lady, remember?"

Between hourly visits, I called our family and three of Jody's closest friends: Dottie McKay, Dorothy McClelland, and Joan Hebert, telling them Jody had made it through the operation and that the prognosis was hopeful.

Three days after the operation, Jody's pulse quickened and her temperature shot up. The doctors were concerned. Jody kept begging for medication to kill the pain. And it was on this day that I saw the stitches —a circuit that ran from the base of her skull down the entire right side of her neck to her throat. But then matters improved. In a few more days the pain had subsided, and she was strong enough to sit up in bed. A week later the doctors said Jody could leave the hospital. We drove home on the Hollywood Freeway, both aware that it was here that Jody had had her accident.

It was during this drive back to our home, where our son Bo was waiting with neighbors to welcome Jody home, that Jody began making plans for a trip. She was anxious to meet a woman she'd never known.

The Squirrel Lady was waiting ... she'd been waiting a long time.

17

JODY WANTED TO CALL her mother immediately, but I urged her to wait awhile. I wanted her to hold off until she was stronger, until it was closer to the time when the doctors would agree that she was well enough to travel to Indiana. I also argued that there was her mother to consider, for until my contact with her, she'd never expected to hear from her daughter, ever. All this would take some getting used to—a reasonable period of adjustment.

Still, a day or so later Jody made the call. When I came home that evening I sensed a change in her mood—and not long after, she was sobbing.

I sat beside her. "What is it, honey?"

"Nothing, nothing at all."

"Why all the tears, then?"

"It's nothing, honest. . . ."

I kissed her. "Come on, Jo, what is it?"

She looked up at me, her eyes filled again with tears.

I waited. Finally Jody spoke. "I called my mother today."

"Oh . . ."

"I wanted so much to talk to her. . . ."

"And?"

"She was polite."

"Then why the tears?"

Jody's lips trembled. "She said we could be friends, but . . . she didn't think it would be a good idea for me to visit her."

"And what did you say?"

"Not much . . . just that I would write to her."

"And. . . ?"

"And then we said goodbye."

"That was all?"

She looked down at the floor. "I shouldn't have called, I guess."

I took Jody into my arms. "Give it some time," I said. "She's . . . well, you know, still bewildered by it all."

But Jody's depression continued and deepened, and the doctors were concerned. The depression could impede her recovery. Her spirits had to be lifted. Maybe, I decided, I could locate her missing brother, her twin. It would help, I was sure. If I had been able to trace Edith Carnahan, perhaps I could find Robert Carnahan. This time, though, I faced one serious obstacle. No leads. In the search for Jody's mother, I had a city to go to. In her brother's case I had only a name and an age: Robert Carnahan, forty-seven. Nothing more. No town, no state, no address.

I called the Los Angeles Social Security Office. The

agent told me to write a letter to Robert Carnahan. It would be sent to Social Security's headquarters in Baltimore. Someday, if they ever found Robert Carnahan, they'd forward the letter. Who knows, maybe he'd respond.

I appreciated the concern for Bob Carnahan's privacy, but something in the man's voice told me the letter might be a long time in getting to him. Besides, there was Jody's health to think of.

So instead of writing a letter, I called my paper's Washington bureau and spoke with news editor Dennis Britton, explaining about Jody's illness and her brother.

"I don't want to involve the paper," I said. "Is there someone who can work on this in their spare time?"

"Sure, we'll give it to Reston," Britton said.

He transferred the call to correspondent Richard Reston, the son of Scotty Reston, famed *New York Times* journalist. Dick Reston took Bob Carnahan's name and said he'd be in touch. He was. He called back thirty minutes later.

"Social Security wants to know if that's all you've got, a name and an age?"

"That's it," I said. "Name, age, period."

"It's not much to go on."

"I know. . . ."

But Reston didn't stop just with Social Security. He made calls to the Pentagon, the Internal Revenue Service, and the FBI. The FBI came up with several leads, but each one involved the wrong Carnahan. It was just as well. I had no great desire for Jody to learn that her brother was a bank-robber or a safe-cracker, certainly not now.

Dick got no feedback from the IRS, but the Pentagon responded with the following information: Robert Carnahan had served with the U.S. Army during World War II, had been wounded in action in New Guinea, and had been awarded the Purple Heart. Beyond that, they knew nothing.

Over the next several days Reston dug up other bits and pieces of information, but each one proved a dead-end. Still he wouldn't quit. I'd spoken to Dick originally on Monday. Now it was Friday. Five days had passed, and although Jody was still ill, I decided to phone Reston when I got to the office and tell him to call off the search. At this point it seemed hopeless. How could we expect to find one human among two hundred and forty million . . . with no leads. Besides, he was doing all this in his spare time, and I felt I was taking advantage.

Then, quite suddenly, everything turned around. As I arrived at the *Times* on Friday morning, receptionist Kathi Barr said I had an urgent message.

"Call Mr. Reston right away," she said.

Reston was excited when he answered the phone.

"Hey, pal, Social Security found your wife's brother!"

"Where?"

"Some whistle stop called Locust Grove." He paused.

"You're kidding! Where's that?"

"You got me. Some place in Oklahoma. Anyway, the guy's supposed to get in touch with you. They gave him your home telephone number."

"How long ago?"

"About an hour, maybe."

"Dick . . . thanks! Dammit, man, thanks!"

I hung up and dialed our house.

The line was busy.

Bob Carnahan wasn't home when the Social Security agent stopped at his trailer. He was helping a neighbor fix the transmission in his car. His wife, Beulah, was gone, too. She was grocery shopping. The agent left a note pinned to their door, instructing Bob to call the Social Security office in Tulsa immediately.

When Carny called, they asked if he knew someone named Helene Jo Hulse.

He thought for a moment. "Don't believe I do," he said at last.

"Well, do you have a sister?" the agent asked.

Bob started to explain. "I do, but . . ."

The agent interrupted. "What is your mother's name?"

"Edith Neukom."

"Where does she live?"

"Auburn, Indiana."

This was information I'd fed to Reston when Social Security pressed him for additional facts.

"Okay," the agent said. "You're the guy."

"But, I don't understand . . ."

The agent explained about Jody, that she was ill and her family was trying to contact him. He gave him our telephone number.

Carny put down the receiver and just sat and stared into space.

Then he tried to speak. "Beulah . . ." And then he jumped up and started shouting. "My sister, Beulah, my sister!"

He scared the woman half to death.

But he just kept on shouting it: "Beulah, my sister! I've found my sister!"

Jody was dozing when the phone rang beside her bed. When she picked it up, she heard a man ask, "Is this Helene Jo Hulse?"

"Yes," she said, still drowsy.

"Well, by golly, I'm not sure how to say this, but this is your brother calling."

There was a long pause, and then Jody said, "Who?"

"Your brother, Robert—"

"Please, is this a joke?"

"By golly, no!"

Now, patiently, her brother explained how he'd gotten the message to call because of her illness, and that he was her blood brother . . . and then he told her he'd been searching for her for more than thirty-five years.

While they were talking, the private nurse we had hired came into the room. Jody was nearly hysterical.

The nurse was alarmed. "What's wrong with you?"

"Nothing, nothing at all," Jody said, smiling hugely, waving the nurse away.

From Oklahoma, Bob Carnahan asked, "Hey, sister, are you all right?"

"I'm fine, I'm fine. . . ." was all Jody could say, and then she was weeping, and Carny, listening to his sister, cried too, and with their tears they were saying all that they needed to say, all that could be said over the miles and miles that separated them and all the years of their lonely lives.

18

Bob Carnahan couldn't afford a trip to California, and so Jody, in time and with the blessings of her doctors, flew to Oklahoma.

As for Bob Carnahan, he was getting ready. On the day of her flight, he was washing the car that was parked alongside his trailer home. Things had to be just right for his sister.

He was whistling a song he'd heard Dolly Parton sing, "Love Is a Butterfly." Then, right in the middle of his favorite verse, he stopped and looked at what was his—the trailer with the little tin awning and a patch of grass. He lived here with Beulah and little Donnie, and it wasn't much, was it? A sick feeling came over him. Would his sister be disappointed? She was a fine lady from Los Angeles. She was flying by jet across the country to come to this. His head throbbed. He tried to force it all from his mind and got out the chamois and began drying the car. He didn't want any water spots.

From the porch, Beulah had been watching, and Carny called out to her. "Donnie getting ready?"

"Been ready an hour," his wife called. "That boy just can't wait to meet his new aunt."

"Neither can I," Carny said, "neither can I."

Beulah Carnahan sighed. "Well, d'you suppose she's one of them snobs?"

"Beulah!"

"Well, I was just wonderin', that's all."

Carny tossed the chamois onto the porch and then stood to one side, inspecting the car. "How's it look?" he shouted to Beulah.

"Looks real fine, Bob."

Inside the trailer, he took great care shining his shoes, laying on extra polish to hide the scuff marks. He put in a pair of new laces.

Then he showered and shaved and got into his best pair of slacks and got out a shirt he'd been saving for something special. He combed his hair very carefully, watching himself in the mirror. Well, he'd better get a move on—it was a fair stretch to Tulsa, a good forty-five, maybe fifty miles, and it wouldn't hurt to get there a few minutes early. He called into the living room, "Beulah, Donnie, let's go!"

"It's only noon," Beulah called back. "Plane don't get here till three o'clock."

"I know, Beulah, I know. Just want to make sure we don't miss it. Could be we have car trouble or something."

But Beulah Carnahan had decided she had to brush

her red hair till it shone, and then she put on her nicest
church dress. That's where she'd wanted to take Bob
on their first date, to church. He'd taken her roller-
skating instead.

This was in Modesto, California, where Carny had
been stationed during World War II. He'd met Beulah
earlier, before going overseas. But it was fourteen
years until he saw her again. The second time was
after the war ... after he'd gone home and things
hadn't worked out in Indiana and so he'd returned to
Modesto. Beulah was working in a restaurant, and she
was still pretty. Only by that time she was a widow
with five kids. He got along with them just fine, and so
he and Beulah got married and he helped rear them.
They were all grown now. Only Donnie was left, and
he was their own. Sometimes Bob got accused of spoil-
ing the boy, but this was because he knew what growing up without a dad was like.

Getting into the car, he noticed that Donnie was
wearing the same clothes he'd worn to his sixth grade
graduation last Friday night ... the same new slacks
and the white shirt and tie. He was a handsome boy,
with Carny's dark eyes and dark hair. He was going to
be a mite taller, though. They were already nearly
head to head, and he was only twelve years old.

Carny swung the car onto the country road leading
down Murphy Hill to the highway, and kept the
needle at sixty, clear to Tulsa.

At Tulsa International Airport, Carny parked the
car and they all went into the terminal. They had to
wait nearly two hours for the plane.

Carny kept getting up and pacing, his stomach still

queasy. Each time he looked at the clock he figured it'd stopped. He and Beulah and Donnie kept watching people coming and going, and then, a few minutes past three, they heard the announcement: "American Airlines Flight 382 from Los Angeles and Oklahoma City is now arriving. Passengers will be disembarking through Gate 33. . . ."

Suddenly there she was—just like the picture she had sent ahead. By golly, she was even prettier than her picture. It was her. It was his sister!

Then Jody saw him and she broke into the biggest grin he'd ever seen and they ran to each other—Jody throwing her arms around Carny, Carny hugging Jody, the tears streaming down his face. They were laughing and crying like they'd never stop, and everybody was looking and smiling and thinking, Now look at that, isn't that something special?

On the drive to Locust Grove the conversation started out slowly, with a few awkward silences, but by the time they'd crossed the Grand River and turned up Murphy Hill, everyone was chattering. All at once.

"Our sons came with us to the airport," Jody was saying.

And then Beulah was saying, "We've got four sons altogether."

Then Donnie was saying: "Guess what, Aunt Jody, I graduated from the sixth grade Friday night."

And then Bob looked in the rearview mirror and said, "Sis, we're just common folks . . . I hope you won't mind none."

And then he started saying how they lived in a

trailer and that he worked at a truck stop, pumping gasoline. He was saying this as he pulled up beside the trailer and switched off the ignition. As he was helping Jody out of the car a curious procession got under way up Murphy Hill. A crowd of neighbors had been peering from behind trees and bushes and now suddenly everyone started shuffling by, gawking and whispering. They'd all heard that Bob Carnahan's sister was visiting from Hollywood, and to these hill folk that meant only one thing: a movie star had come to Locust Grove.

Bob had tried to explain but it was useless. Some even asked Jody for her autograph. Even Old Man Tugman, who shot at neighbors and was usually raising all sorts of cain.

"Sure is purty," Old Man Tugman said.

Bob led Jody to the trailer. "This is where we live, Sis. I hope you're not too disappointed."

"Oh, Bob, I love it."

Jody saw the chickens and the ducks running in the yard and the horses grazing in the pasture, and she smiled happily at the faces she saw all around her, at Beulah and at Donnie and at her twin brother, Bob.

Jody was more at ease and more content those next few weeks than she had ever been before in her life. Bob called her "Sis" and "Sissy," and when Donnie learned his Aunt Jody could blow bubbles (he provided the gum), she became his favorite aunt—Aunt Jody. She and Donnie went picnicking under skies so blue they hurt your eyes. They made a lunch of potato chips, candy, and soda pop, hardly a diet for a woman who'd been on the edge of death only weeks before. Doctor Marxer was right ... the mind works miracles over the body.

Jody learned to bait a hook and they all went fishing from the banks of the Grand. Bob would clean the fish and Beulah cooked them, and Jody sat and watched the moon come up and wished these days could go on forever. After dinner Donnie would get out his telescope and they'd gaze at the stars—although all anyone had to do was just look up, because the stars hang low and shine brightly in those Oklahoma heavens during summer. Then they would sit listening to the locusts and eating watermelon until it was late and the moon was gone and it was time to turn in—in a little place off in the hills called Locust Grove.

19

It was a few days after Jody had returned from Oklahoma that the call came. It was dinnertime, and when Jody answered the telephone, the soft Midwestern voice said, "May I speak to Jody?"

I heard the way my wife said "This is Jody," and I knew who it had to be.

The call was from Auburn, of course.

It was time now. Edith Neukom was ready—so would Jody please arrange to visit?

Oh, yes . . . yes, of course!

After several more telephone calls and an exchange of letters, Jody decided on a date in September. Her doctors wanted her to get plenty of rest first. They wanted her to have all the happiness she could get, but they also wanted her to explore it at a more leisurely pace.

Jody remained obsessed with self-doubts. One night she asked, "Do you suppose she'll like me?"

"Your mother, honey?" I put my arms around my wife. "Jo, she'll love you just as we all do."

Jody looked up at me. "I hope so. I've never hoped for anything so much in my life."

As the day of Jody's departure neared, she became progressively more nervous. She wanted to "look just right," she said, "for my mother."

She'd choose what she'd wear on the airplane, then she'd change her mind again. Over and over, she kept redoing everything, fretting over the smallest detail. She'd been to the beauty shop and she looked lovelier than I could ever remember. All that remained of her brush with death was the red scar which angled down her neck from her ear to her throat.

And then the day came.

She'd been up since dawn, Jody admitted as we drove to the airport.

"I couldn't sleep," she said, "I just couldn't."

The traffic was horrendous. Everyone, it seemed, was on the freeway with us, all headed in the same direction. The streets—and especially the San Diego Freeway, which we were traveling—were clogged bumper-to-bumper. I checked my watch. Seven thirty. We had plenty of time. Her flight wouldn't be leaving for another hour.

Later, inside the terminal, a skycap checked Jody's luggage and we went over to the snack counter for coffee. But Jody couldn't drink hers—she was too nervous.

At the gate, I kissed Jody goodbye. She looked up at me. "Thank you," she said simply. "Thank you for giving me my mother."

Then she turned and hurried onto the plane.

At cruising altitude, a stewardess stopped to visit.

"You look awfully excited," she told Jody.

Jody smiled. "I am."

"What's the occasion?"

Jody beamed again. "I'm going to meet my mother ... for the first time."

"Aw, c'mon."

"Honestly."

The stewardess slid into an empty seat beside her as Jody proceeded to recount the entire story, every detail of it, from blacking out on the freeway more than a dozen weeks earlier to being aboard this airplane on her way to meet her mother. When Jody was finished, the stewardess sat shaking her head, eyes glistening.

Jody was too excited to read, so she took out the picture of her mother. She studied the photo. They resembled each other, Jody thought, something about the mouth; the eyes too, although the colors were different. Maybe it was their shape.

Would she recognize her mother?

She looked at her watch. One fifteen, L.A. time. She moved the hands forward to the proper hour— three fifteen. She would be changing planes in Chicago soon. Already the stewardesses were passing out the passengers' belongings.

In Chicago Jody had a forty-five minute wait for her flight to Fort Wayne—and she used all that time to worry and wonder. She sat for several minutes in the passenger lounge. Then she got up and paced. What should she say? *Hello, Mother? Hello, Mom? Hello, Edith?* No, she'd never call her mother by her first name. She'd heard others do that and it sounded disrespectful. Well, she'd just let the moment of their meeting take care of itself.

After what seemed hours, Jody heard her flight being called. Her pulse quickened. In exactly one hour she'd be in Fort Wayne.

And then she was airborne, and the hour passed at the pace of a century, weighed down by the burden of a million billion moments of longing and all the dreams a child can ever have. And then the plane touched down in Fort Wayne and it rolled forever and then it drew to a halt and Jody pressed through the other passengers and ran all the way to the terminal.

It wasn't until she was inside the terminal that she saw her, the tiny woman standing alone in the crowd ... so small she was barely visible.

Their eyes met. A smile came to the woman's lips and she began walking toward Jody. Suddenly it struck Jody ... suddenly she realized who this woman was. Jody dropped her handbag and ran. And then she was in her mother's arms, for the first time in her life she was in her mother's arms, and her mother was whispering over and over, "Oh, my darling baby, I'm so sorry, so sorry. . . ."

Jody held the tiny woman, hugging her, whispering back, "Please, please, Mother, don't be sorry."

EPILOGUE

Yesterday is gone.

Tomorrow? Well, never mind....

But today? This is all that counts.... It's all that counts, really.

Jody no longer dwells on the memories of all the yesterdays she had.

In order to survive, to continue living, Jody requires medication. Daily. It offers no guarantees, and so she counts only on *this* day, this moment; and it is precious. She is sure only of the present, for she can see it (the blue of the heavens), smell it (the roses in our yard and Katy's, next door), hear it (the crash of the surf and the rush of the wind).

On our mantel there is a little plastic statue. It shows a girl and a boy standing together, arms locked around each other, and below the figures an inscription reads: "Love isn't love until it's shared."

It was a gift from Bob.

And sitting on a shelf in an antique knickknack cabinet—not far as your eyes sweep away from the girl and boy on the mantel—can be seen the bright colors of a dishcloth, carefully folded, its layers lying smoothly, one atop the other.

All our lives have changed—Jody's, Mom Neukom's, Bob Carnahan's, mine. I know now how fragile love can be, the spaces that can open in a marriage, and how constantly it begs attention. There is no making up for the lost years, but no one can stop us from trying. Bob, who'd never had an Easter basket, got one last year. Jody spent hours coloring eggs and stuffing the basket with chocolate candy. Absurd, you say? A grown man getting the Easter basket he'd always wanted? Not really. Sad, perhaps—but not absurd. And Bob Carnahan ate every last egg.

He keeps all of Jody's letters. He has them tied in a bundle and locked in a closet. When he dies he wants those letters buried with him. It's a big bundle.

Bob doesn't live in Oklahoma any more. He and Beulah and Donnie live in Palm Springs now. Down with all the movie stars. He works at Tamarisk Country Club repairing golf carts, and they all come to see us whenever they can.

Mom Neukom spends a lot of time on her front porch these days, watching for her mail carrier. He's always either bringing a letter signed "Love, Jody," or carrying off one signed "Your loving mom."

As for Jody, I can hear her now. She's outside waiting for our letter carrier . . . and she's whistling. A long time ago, when we were very young, she whistled constantly. People on the street would stop and listen because she whistled so beautifully.

Sometimes the birds would hear her and they'd whistle too. But this was a long time ago. And then of course our lives changed, and she stopped whistling. Until now.

So, like I say, she's outside whistling with the sparrows and the robins, waiting for the mailman.

He never rings here any more. He doesn't have to. Jody is always there ahead of him, standing next to the mailbox, waiting to see if she's gotten a letter from her mother . . . or her brother . . . or a sister-in-law . . . a cousin . . . a niece . . . a nephew . . . an aunt . . . an uncle . . . .